The Prickly Pear Cookbook

RIO NUEVO PUBLISHERS
P.O. Box 5250, Tucson, Arizona 85703-0250
(520) 623-9558, www.rionuevo.com

Cover design by David Jenney, Flagstaff, Arizona
Interior design by Karen Schober, Seattle, Washington
Food styling by Tracy Vega

Library of Congress Cataloging-in-Publication Data

Niethammer, Carolyn J.
  The prickly pear cookbook / by Carolyn Niethammer.
     p. cm.
Includes index.
  ISBN 1-887896-56-2
  1. Cookery, International. 2. Prickly pears. I. Title.
  TX725.A1N54 2004
  641.6'4775--dc22
                                        2003022277

Printed in Korea
10 9 8 7 6

The
Prickly Pear
Cookbook

Carolyn Niethammer

photography by Robin Stancliff

RIO NUEVO
PUBLISHERS

Tucson, Arizona

CONTENTS

INTRODUCTION

Here we go round the prickly pear
Prickly pear prickly pear
Here we go round the prickly pear
At five o'clock in the morning.

—from *"The Hollow Men" by T. S. Eliot*

Over the past few millennia, the succulent pads and juicy sweet fruits of the prickly pear cactus have fed millions of humans and other animals, offering life-sustaining calories, vitamins, calcium, and a host of other minerals. Today top chefs in many parts of the world include the pads and fruit in dishes served in elegant restaurants.

Yet throughout history prickly pears have also been seen as ominous. O. Henry wrote about the prickly pear in his story "The Caballero's Way":

Spring is the season for gathering tender, succulent new prickly pear pads before the big thorns have developed. Pictured is the Santa Rita cactus, but pads of all varieties are edible and are easily processed into tasty, nutritious dishes enjoyed by millions of people worldwide.

More weird and lonesome than the journey of an Amazonian explorer is the ride...through a Texas pear flat. With dismal monotony and startling variety, the uncanny and multiform shapes of the cacti lift their twisted trunks and fat bristly hands to encumber the way. The demon plant, appearing to live without soil or rain, seems to taunt the parched traveler with its lush grey greenness.

That parched traveler would have been better off had he stopped to pick one of the fruits or pads and cleaned it with his knife for a refreshing snack. Both pads and fruit are between 85 and 90 percent water.

The prickly pear plant, of the genus *Opuntia,* is native to the Americas from Chile to Canada. A remnant population lingers on an island off the shore of Connecticut (the original larger stand disappeared after being over-collected by the Victorians for their terrariums).

Columbus took the plant back to Europe at the end of the fifteenth century, and from there it has spread all over the planet. It was already so prominent in Italy by the seventeenth century that the sculptor Giovanni Lorenzo Bernini included a depiction of the prickly pear cactus in a fountain he designed for the Piazza Navona in Rome around 1650.

In each land where the cactus took root, the inhabitants have formed their own name for the sweet, usually egg-shaped fruit. In Mesoamerica, where they are especially abundant, the Mexicans call the fruits *tunas.* To the English they are Indian figs, to the French, Barberry figs, to the Italians, *fichidindia,* and to the Spanish, *higos chumbos.* The Greeks call the fruit *barbarosikia* ("fig of the foreigners"), and in the Holy Land the name is *sabur* or *subbar* in Arabic and *tzabar* (anglicized to *sabra*) in Hebrew. In the eastern zone of Tigray, in northern Ethiopia, we can find forty-eight words for different varieties of prickly pear in the language Erob Woreda—including *gabaile* (cactus inhabited by snakes), *ourgufa* (cactus with fruits that fall down early), and *kari-hada* (cactus loved by dogs but not consumed by humans).

The prickly pear is deeply embedded in the culture of Mexico, appearing on its coat of arms and national flag. Folklore describes how the Aztecs, after wandering for many generations looking for a home, one day saw an eagle perched on a prickly pear cactus on a small swampy island in the lake of Texcoco. Taking this as a sign of where they should settle, the Aztecs (also called the Mexica) in A.D. 1325 built a city they named México-Tenochtitlán, meaning "In the moon's navel—place of the prickly pear cactus." This location is near the center of today's Mexico City.

Unfortunately, in some areas like Australia, India, and South Africa, the prickly pear has made itself so much at home that it is threatening the ecological balance and crowding out the native plants. These countries are having to use whatever biological and mechanical means they can come up with to keep the spread of the plants in check.

PRICKLY PEARS AS FOOD Prickly pear fruits were the first wild food I ever gathered. I was a youngster, about ten or eleven years old, and my parents were Midwestern transplants to northern Arizona. They loved to put my brother and me in the back of the Jeep and head off to explore whatever back roads we could get to on a day trip. Somebody must have told them about prickly pears, because one afternoon in early fall, we stopped on what I remember as a very curvy dirt road near Oak Creek Canyon, near a cluster of knee- to waist-high prickly pear plants. We used tongs to pick the stickery cactus fruits, licking some of the sweet juice off our fingers when the fruit was punctured. We then deposited them in a brown paper bag that immediately became stained with the bright purple juice. In my memory the sky was deep Dutch blue and the sun golden.

My mother used to recall how the smell of apples spelled autumn for her in Illinois, where she grew up. But from that perfect day on, for me the fragrance of sun-warmed prickly pear fruits became one of the defining memories of fall. Later, when I moved to southern Arizona, I noticed that in the lower-elevation deserts, prickly pear fruit begins to ripen by mid-summer, although some plants—usually those in city gardens—retain their fruit into autumn. Out in the deserts and forests, the local critters are quick to devour the fruits as soon as they ripen. On a recent fall afternoon, I was hiking with friends in a canyon in the Chiricahua Mountains in southeastern Arizona and noticed large piles of magenta-colored scat—bears eating prickly pear fruit, my friends explained. Given the competition from everything from little rock squirrels and birds to bears, we two-legged "desert rats" have to scurry to get our share of sweet prickly pears too. Fortunately, there always seems to be plenty to go around.

What does prickly pear fruit taste like? The flavor depends on the variety, ranging from comparison to watermelon or honeydew melon, to berry-like, or a bit like cucumbers. Some are rather sour; others, like the Engelmann, have slightly musky flavor notes unlike anything I've tasted elsewhere.

Not all prickly pear fruits are red—they also come in green, like the large one pictured here, as well as yellow and orange. Popular Latin ingredients also shown here: tomatillos (above and below the prickly pear), limes, and the pungent herb cilantro (top of picture).

Prickly pear was eaten in the Americas as far back as 65 B.C. and possibly earlier. When Cabeza de Vaca was exploring the coast of what is now Texas and ended up lost for many years, he accompanied the local Indians on a cactus-gathering trip and described how they squeezed the juice from the fruits and drank it. Southwestern indigenous people's traditional diets have also long included saguaro fruits, cholla buds, agave hearts, and many other desert foods.

Today, Mexicans are the leading producers and consumers of prickly pear cactus, having more than twenty times the acreage of Italy, their nearest competitor. Mexican shoppers are sophisticated consumers of prickly pear fruits, knowing exactly which varieties they prefer. While most other people consume only the fruit, Mexicans also relish the green pads, calling them *nopales* or *pencas* when whole and *nopalitos* when cut into small pieces. They have a very mild vegetable flavor with a slight lemony zip. Although they are widely available in jars, they are best eaten fresh, cooked in one of the ways found on pages 26 and 27. In some households they are a daily staple food, made into a simple salad, grilled and wrapped in a tortilla, or cooked into more elaborate dishes such as the recipes given in this book.

Some species of the genus *Opuntia* produce tastier pads; others are better for fruits. In Mexico and throughout the world, extensive plant-breeding programs aim at producing even more palatable varieties. Fruits come in a rainbow of colors—white, green, yellow, orange, red, purple, and brown. Preferences are mainly cultural: Mexicans have the greatest range of commercial varieties. They relish the more rare pale-skinned varieties and judge quality by viscosity, amount of acid, color, number of stickers, seed-to-pulp ratio, and the size of the seeds. Italians have fewer choices, though Northern Italians prefer yellow fruits, while Southern Italians prefer red. People in the Southwestern United States are used to the deep-magenta fruits of the wild Engelmann prickly pear.

Engelmann is also the variety used by commercial producers of prickly pear syrup and candies such as Cheri's Desert Harvest and Cahill's, and of the unsweetened juice from Arizona Cactus Ranch. The availability of prickly pear syrup has led to the country-wide passion for prickly pear margaritas. If all you've tasted are the bottled syrups, however, you are missing the fragrance of a sun-warmed cactus fruit—and some of the pleasure. Commercial syrups, while delicious, are necessarily highly processed, and some of the subtlety of the flavors is lost.

In many parts of the world, fresh prickly pears are street food, sold curbside or by market vendors and eaten immediately. An anthropologist writing in 1907 described a market in Zacatecas, Mexico, where women would arrive with huge baskets of tunas. Each purchaser was given the tip of a maguey leaf (magueys are related to century plants) or a mesquite thorn to hold the fruit while they ate it. Typically today the vendor will cut off the two ends of the fruit and slit it down one side, peeling back the skin, stickers and all, for the customer to eat on the spot.

About 90 percent of Italy's prickly pear fruits are grown on Sicily. Italians prefer the tall *Opuntia ficus indica,* which has fewer thorns. Many of the fruits are exported to other areas of Italy and other European countries, but Sicilians greatly enjoy them, and in the past the poorest inhabitants of the island subsisted on them for three to four months of the year. Today the average Sicilian eats about five pounds of fichidindia annually.

In Mary Taylor Simeti's book *On Persephone's Island*—a memoir of the author's life on Sicily—she describes prickly pears as "bright ovals of fuchsia, chartreuse, and yellow, extracted from their spiny skins and heaped upon a platter. Dearly beloved part of the Sicilian summer, they are very delicate, difficult to gather, and easy to bruise." They were as important as the tomatoes, melons, and grapes of the season. She explains that to pick them, one must

Commercial syrups and jellies provide shortcuts to cooking with prickly pear fruit.

place a grape leaf in the palm of the hand like a potholder, while with the other hand one cuts it from the cactus. Those that are to be eaten right away should be taken to the kitchen in a bucket of water and skinned. Those to be given as a gift must be placed in a wicker basket lined with grape leaves and covered with another layer of leaves.

Prickly pears have even made it as far as Asia and are being grown commercially for the fruit in China, Vietnam, and Cambodia.

NUTRITION The nutritional value of the pads and fruits varies according to the species, growing conditions, season, age of the plant, and harvesting conditions. In general, the pads are about 90 percent water, with decent amounts of vitamin C and beta-carotene and very little carbohydrate or fat. The fruit is about 85 percent water, with from 10 to 15 percent carbohydrates, 6 to 8 percent glucose and fructose, and about 25 to 30 calories in a quarter pound. They also offer substantial amounts of calcium and vitamins C and A. Among the poor of Mexico, the tunas and nopales are an important source of vitamins.

According to University of Arizona ethnohistorian Tom Sheridan, the Spanish conquistadors recognized the benefits of the prickly pear as a partial cure for the scurvy that plagued their sailors. They didn't understand about vitamin C, but they were aware that like most fresh fruits, the native people's tunas kept them healthier.

PRICKLY PEARS AS MEDICINE For generations, the prickly pear has played an important role in the pharmacopoeia of native healers in Mexican and Southwestern Native American tribes. An Aztec herbal book from 1552 included a picture of a prickly pear pad and a prescription for a burn ointment that combines nopal juice, honey, and egg yolk. When the plant was spread to other parts of the world after being discovered by Spanish explorers, healers around the world began discovering its healthful properties and incorporated both the pads and fruits into their practices.

The sap of the pads is similar to that of aloe and can soothe irritated skin. Aztecs used the sap to expel intestinal parasites and to increase the excretion of urine. It has been used widely for wounds, burns, and sunburn by Native American tribes and in the Bahamas and China. In Sicily it was used traditionally to reduce the itch of measles, in Sri Lanka and India it has been used on boils, and in China a split pad was bound on dog bites. Women in China and Sri Lanka and among the Pima Indians of Arizona have used heated split pads to soothe breasts sore from nursing. In Central Africa sap from the pads has been used as a mosquito repellent.

In the 1850s a Texas Ranger put prickly pear poultices on wounds his men had sustained in a battle with the Comanches. When the post surgeon saw this "primitive" treatment, he removed the poultices, and the wounds got worse. The Ranger reapplied the cactus, and his men recovered rapidly.

Other uses of more dubious value were for gout, tumors, hair loss, pimples, warts, gonorrhea, syphilis, tuberculosis, malaise, and insomnia.

PRICKLY PEAR AND DIABETES One common medical use in Mexico today is as a treatment for diabetics. While this might seem a farfetched claim for a stickery plant that grows in the desert, clinical studies have shown that prickly pear can indeed help regulate the blood sugar of people suffering from this disease. Several groups of prestigious Mexican medical researchers have been investigating prickly pear pads since the mid-1980s. A few studies have also been done in the United States. After conducting studies on dogs, rabbits, rats, and guinea pigs, the scientists tried their experiments on humans. The researchers confirmed their hypothesis: that eating prickly pear cactus pads can help regulate blood glucose levels in human beings with non-insulin-dependent diabetes mellitus (NIDDM).

The researchers noticed a significant benefit in just two hours after the meals and even more improvement after four and six hours. The response in the research subjects can be partly explained by the high fiber content of the pads. The pads contain two to three times the amount of dietary fiber—both soluble and nonsoluble—found in wheat bran and oats. This comes in the form of cellulose, pectin, gums, and mucilage.

Texas prickly pear (Opuntia engelmannii, *var.* lindheimeri), *Perez Ranch, Texas.*

But that's not the whole story. There is something else going on that the researchers haven't yet been able to figure out. Prickly pear seems to increase sensitivity to insulin through some unexplained process. Even more interesting, there were no changes in the glucose levels of the research subjects who did not have diabetes.

Other studies have shown that prickly pear pads can reduce the blood levels of triglycerides, total cholesterol, and low-density lipoprotein (LDL) cholesterol in the research subjects. There was no change in the level of the high-density lipoprotein (HDL), the "good" cholesterol.

In the various studies, subjects ate anywhere from fifty to five hundred grams of nopales. Five hundred grams is about a pound—quite a lot of nopales to eat unless you are extraordinarily fond of them. A more reasonable study had participants eat one hundred grams before each meal. That's just two pads the size of a small woman's hand. In some cases the nopales were liquefied, which might have been easier for the subjects, although the drink would have been rather viscous.

Although one study maintained that the viscosity or stickiness of the sap played an important role in the responses, in later studies the subjects were given nopales that were variously warm, cold, raw, or broiled. All gave the same physiologic response. Pads that have been broiled are less sticky, but they have not lost anything but water. Nopales prepared by boiling and then rinsed to reduce the viscosity would apparently be less helpful, because much of the sap will have been washed away. It made no difference in the studies what time of year the pads were gathered. However, several experiments have shown that the dried powdered nopales sold in Mexico in capsules are not effective in reducing either cholesterol or blood sugar.

Dr. Michael Friedman, a naturopathic physician practicing in Connecticut, reports excellent results in treating his NIDDM patients with capsules containing prickly pear cactus stems in the form of dried powder mixed with other herbs. He has also used the capsules to treat patients with Syndrome X, a group of health problems that can include insulin resistance (the inability to properly deal with dietary carbohydrates and sugars), abnormal blood fats (such as elevated cholesterol and triglycerides), overweight, and high blood pressure.

"I have found that the more the patient takes, the better the result," he says. "I have seen some diabetics achieve normal blood-sugar readings after a year of taking nopal in combination with other herbs, to the point that they don't even need any herbs anymore and still have normal blood sugar readings. However, I have found that nopal has no positive effect on Diabetes Type 1."

Dr. Friedman conducted a two-year multi-center clinical study of botanicals in diabetes. The results showed that the nopal-herbal combination could lower diabetics' blood sugar by 33 percent within a three-month period.

Natural-health practitioners have gathered a great deal of anecdotal information suggesting that prickly pear fruits and fruit juice are as beneficial as the pads. However, it appears that no medical studies with human subjects have been done on the juice. The Yaqui Indians, who live in Northern Mexico and Southern Arizona, have traditionally used the fruit juice to treat diabetes, and at a Tucson medical clinic serving the Pascua Yaquis, it is routinely given to patients with NIDDM. Dr. Scott L. Jamieson, a Tucson naturopathic doctor who formerly worked at this clinic, has recommended anything from a teaspoon twice a day up to four to six tablespoons of unsweetened prickly pear juice a day with good results. He even prescribes it for patients whose disease is not being totally controlled by insulin and finds that it usually helps.

The juice used at the clinic comes from a business run by Natalie McGee, who processes and bottles the juice without sugar. McGee, who lives in Southern Arizona on forty square miles of desert that her grandfather home-

steaded, is surrounded by Engelmann prickly pears and not much else, other than a few mesquite trees. A few years ago she made some prickly pear products to sell at a local fair and was surprised when people who bought her jams called to tell her they made them feel better and they wanted more. Today McGee gathers fifteen tons of cactus pears every August and September on what she now calls her Arizona Cactus Ranch. Using modern processing, she bottles untold quarts of unsweetened prickly pear nectar that she sells through health food stores in Arizona and through the Internet.

It goes without saying that those who decide to experiment with prickly pears for health reasons should keep a close watch on their blood sugar levels and consult with their doctors.

OTHER RECENT RESEARCH Drug researchers are looking at other traditional medical uses for prickly pear. Parts of the plant have been used by Mexicans, Native Americans, and Sicilians for male urinary discomforts and kidney problems. Recent studies have shown that cactus flower extracts are sometimes helpful for men with benign prostatic hyperplasia (enlarged prostate), although the active ingredients and exactly how they work are not yet clear. In a small clinical trial in Israel, eighty-eight patients took gelatin capsules containing dried cactus flowers. Some of them reported a decreased urgency to urinate and lessening of other symptoms.

Another company is selling a product called Prepair made from an extract of the skin of the *Opuntia ficus indica,* the tall and relatively spineless variety of prickly pear. A French research scientist, Gilles Gutierrez, initially conducted lab tests using rats, in which the extract inhibited experimentally induced joint inflammation and chronic joint inflammation. It also significantly increased wound healing, he reported. The manufacturers of Prepair say that the extract contains a substance that induces the production of proteins that help the

Chef Janos Wilder's Romaine and Nopalito Salad with Oranges and Queso Blanco (see page 57 for recipe).

body respond to physical, psychological, and biological stress. After conducting ten small studies of cyclists, joggers, and scuba divers, the manufacturers of the extract concluded that athletes are able to work out longer and harder while using this patented extract and that the product sped their recoveries from strenuous exercise by in some way accelerating the production of the body's natural restorative compounds.

ANIMAL FEED, GLUE, AND DYE The ability of the *Opuntia* species to grow with very little water once established has made it a good emergency food for livestock and poultry, and much of the current research in southern Europe and South America deals with this use.

Because the pads contain so much water, during droughts prickly pear can keep sheep and cattle alive when grass and other forage is nowhere to be found. Reports say that sheep can live on them for eight months while cattle do better if they have a little supplementary cottonseed meal. The problem with most wild prickly pear plants is that they have long sharp thorns. When cattlemen or sheepherders want their animals to eat the plants, they usually help them out by burning off the stickers. Bill and Sarah Maltsberger, who raise cattle on a 15,000-acre ranch in the dry lands between San Antonio and Laredo, Texas, figure they can fill a cow up on prickly pear for about six cents a day, the cost for propane to burn the needles off the pads. The Maltsbergers also stress that prickly pear plants can be planted and left on their own until needed in dry times, unlike grass, which can't be stockpiled.

The great plant breeder Luther Burbank worked from 1906 to 1915 to develop a number of varieties of spineless cactus to make things easier for the stockmen, but the cactus tend to revert to spininess when grown in the wild.

Mexican dairy farmers particularly like to feed prickly pear pads to their stock, because they give a distinctive and highly desired flavor to the milk and butter. The farmers and cactus growers barter pads for manure. Many owners of reptiles buy or gather prickly pear pads and fruits for their pets. Tortoises presumably like the sweetness and bright color of the fruit.

In addition to its use as animal food, the prickly pear shows up in many other products. The stickiness of the sap helps in making products such as chewing gum and candles, and it can serve as a stiffening agent for cotton cloth. In 1911, Burbank wrote an article in *Scientific American* reporting that when prickly pear sap is spread on water, it smothers mosquito larvae—an effect that can last up to a year. A common use of the sap in rural areas of Mexico is to boil it down into a concentrate and mix it with whitewash and mortar to increase the durability of buildings. When Mexican restorers periodically come to work on the two-hundred-year-old frescos in the mission church at Tumacácori, south of Tucson, Arizona, they use a product containing prickly pear sap to glue back the tiny chips that have fallen off.

It has also helped significantly in the restoration of the 1783 Mission San Xavier del Bac just outside of Tucson. Architects determined that twentieth-century products used to stabilize the building were actually contributing to its deterioration. They decided to go back to the original plaster, in which lime and sand—bound by mucilage extracted from the prickly pear cactus—were applied as a "breathing" protective coating. To obtain the mucilage, the builders boiled pads of prickly pear cactus in large kettles and mashed them to get the gooey extract that they then mixed with the mortar.

A major commercial use of the prickly pear is for red pigments, which were particularly important before the advent of synthetic dyes. The female cochineal insect feeds on the pads and fruits and produces carminic acid, which is used to make a brilliant magenta dye. The Aztecs used this to produce the royal red robes of their emperors. Spanish explorers were much taken with the brilliant color and imported both the dye and the plants, setting up plantations on the Canary Islands for raising the insects. Today the dye is used as a natural coloring for food and as a stain for preparing microscope slides.

CULTIVATION   Plants in the *Opuntia* family are among the easiest ones to grow. The quickest way to get a plant is to start with a pad or two (scientists call them cladodes) of the variety you want to propagate. Allow the cut where you've removed it from the mother plant to form a callus, then plant your cutting one inch deep in a mixture of soil and sand. Put a small stick next

Young prickly pear pads have small rubbery leaves in front of the stickers; as the pad matures, the leaves fall off and the stickers grow. Shown here, a fresh new pad on an Indian fig cactus (Opuntia ficus-indica).

to it for support it until it grows roots. Protect the new plant from the harsh summer sun, and don't water it for a month until it has grown some roots.

Although prickly pears grow fine without fertilizer, if you want fast growth give your plant a high-nitrogen fertilizer. If you want more flowers— leading to more fruit—fertilize once a month throughout the year with a no-nitrogen fertilizer like 0–10–10. Blossoms usually appear on two-year-old pads, although the commercial cactus grower John Dicus says he has gotten a first-year bloom on the variety he calls 'Nopalea Grande,' when the plants receive the proper water and nutrients.

Prickly pear farmers like to extend the season for their fruit so an abundance all at one time doesn't depress the price. Some do this by removing the first flowers to appear in the spring. This practice, called *scozzolatura* in Italy, stimulates a second blooming, and subsequently the fruits on those plants ripen later than the naturally blooming ones, lengthening the season. It is generally accepted that these later fruits (called *bastarduna*) are larger and tastier than the early ones. Farmers also try to control the time of fruiting and vegetative growth by shading.

Like most fruits, prickly pears are highly perishable, having a maximum shelf life of only eight or nine days once picked, a bit longer if refrigerated.

PRICKLY PEARS TODAY   The prickly pear, by virtue of its delicious flavor and the modern diner's quest for exotic foods, has been adopted by top chefs, some of whose recipes appear on the following pages. Once you learn the techniques for dispensing with the stickers on both the pads and fruits, you'll find it easy to prepare the recipes here or to include the cactus in your own favorite dishes.

If you don't live in a part of the world where you can grow your own prickly pears, you can usually find the pads and fruits in a market that caters to Hispanic shoppers, or you can order fresh pads or prickly pear juice or syrup from the sources listed at the end of this book.

In some states, it is against the law to pick the pads of prickly pears growing in the wild, although fruits growing anywhere and pads domesticated in someone's yard are legal. Check the laws in your state.

Only a few decades ago, Italians called prickly pear "the poor man's bread," because the fruit was free or very inexpensive and could be used in so many ways, while the pads made excellent animal fodder. Today, we consider both the pads and fruit a gourmet delicacy, and they are used by some of the most talented professional chefs in the world. So get out your tongs and fill a bucket or a basket with prickly pear fruits or pads, and try some of the marvelous recipes developed by these inventive chefs. *Bon appétit!*

Plains prickly pear (Opuntia macrorhiza), *Buffalo, Texas.*

THE BASICS
PRICKLY PEAR CACTUS PADS

HARVESTING AND CLEANING THE PADS Prickly pear pads or nopales are modified plant stems, and the stickers and tiny rubbery projections near them are modified leaves. The large, longish stickers are called spines and the tiny, hairier ones are glochids. The glochids cause the most trouble as they are so numerous and also have tiny barbs on the end. If you are harvesting your own prickly pear pads, gather newly grown pads in the spring. Pads from wild varieties should be about the size of a small woman's hand—about six inches long; domestic varieties can grow larger, to about the size of a large man's hand—say seven and a half inches—or a little larger. The large Mexican varieties and some types developed by Luther Burbank have fewer stickers. If you have access to them, they are preferable. In any case, the stickers on the young pads are smaller and less lethal than those on the mature ones.

Holding the pads with heavy leather gloves or tongs, cut the pads from the mother plant, leaving about an inch of growth on the plant. New pads will grow from this stump.

Lay the pads flat and, using a serrated steak knife, scrape against the grain of the stickers to remove them. You may have to use the tip of the knife to remove some of the glochids at the base. Some of the newer varieties have so few stickers that you can clean them simply by rubbing with the scrubber side of a kitchen sponge. Trim a thin margin from the outer edge of the cactus. Rinse well and check closely under a strong light for remaining stickers.

"Canned" nopalitos (chopped or sliced prickly pear pads) are also available. They generally come pickled in jars. They are an acquired taste and, unless you really like them, are not suitable for any of the dishes in this book other than the Easy Nopalito Prickly Pear Salsa.

PREPARING THE FRESH PADS FOR RECIPES Professional chefs who work frequently with nopales have devised various methods to deal with what the popular restaurateur and cookbook author Rick Bayless terms "textural challenges." When cut, the pads exude a slippery juice similar to okra. This substance is caused by mucopolysaccharides—a $50 word for a group of complex sugars—and is broken down by weak acids such as vinegar, lemon juice, and tomatoes, and by heat. Studies show, however, that many of the health benefits of the pads come from this juice.

Some cactus aficionados actually embrace the gooey substance. John Dicus, a cactus grower, has a favorite recipe he calls "Dog Drool Salsa," and someone actually entered a recipe for a drink called "Slime Ball on the Beach" in the Texas Cactus Council cooking contest. Should you wish to avoid this substance in your dishes, the juices are easily evaporated by one of the following methods:

Professional chefs such as Alan Zeman are now selling their own products made with prickly pear.

THE RICK BAYLESS METHOD Bayless cleans the pads, dices them into ¾-inch chunks, and tosses them with a little olive oil to coat. He then spreads them on a baking sheet, sprinkles them with a little salt, and roasts them in a 375-degree oven for about 20 minutes. The sticky liquid evaporates, leaving a slightly crisp product.

THE DIANA KENNEDY METHOD Diana Kennedy, who lives in Michoacán, Mexico, has been teaching Mexican cooking since 1969 and has published numerous excellent Mexican cookbooks. She writes in *My Mexico, a Culinary Odyssey,* that she eliminates most of the viscosity in nopales by cooking them *al vapour* or in their own juice. Here's her method:

Heat 1 tablespoon of vegetable oil in a heavy frying pan, add cleaned and diced cactus pieces and a little water, cover, and steam over medium heat for about 5 minutes. Uncover and cook about another 10 minutes, scraping the bottom of the pan to prevent sticking until the liquid is evaporated.

THE DÁVILA GRILL METHOD Suzana Dávila, chef-owner of Café Poca Cosa in Tucson, Arizona, cooks cleaned, oiled prickly pear pads on a hot grill for two or three minutes per side. They will take on an olive green hue and brown slightly. Dávila likes the grill marks and features them in some presentations.

THE PATRICIA QUINTANA METHOD Patricia Quintana is the chef-owner of Izote restaurant in Mexico City and is among the top Mexican cookbook authors writing in English. She suggests putting fresh corn husks and the papery husks of tomatillos in the water when boiling the nopalitos to help cut the slippery juice.

DAVID'S GRANDMOTHER'S METHOD David Eppele, the late owner of Arizona Cactus and Succulent Research, learned to cook cactus from his grandmother Amanda Gutierrez in Socorro, New Mexico. Amanda put the nopalitos in a skillet in a cold oven and brought the temperature slowly up to 350 degrees over 15 minutes. She then transferred the nopalitos to a colander and washed them in very cold water to drain as much of the slippery juice as possible. After draining, she returned them to the skillet and cooked them on the top of the stove—in her case, with bacon and onions.

PRICKLY PEAR FRUITS

HARVESTING AND CLEANING THE FRUITS Prickly pear plants are notorious crossbreeders, so even plant experts can have a hard time telling the exact variety of a plant. In looking for good fruit, you can go by taste and smell. Dark red is usually good, although the fruit on the tall Mexican varieties comes in yellow or green, sometimes with a pale-pinkish tinge. The bigger the individual fruits, the less work for you. Using tongs or heavy leather gloves, pick a fruit and make a small incision with a knife. Squeeze the fruit and taste some of the juice with your finger. If it is sweet, pick more.

In addition to tongs or gloves, two items are essential for working with prickly pears: good, fine tweezers and a stiff vegetable brush. You are going to get stickers in your fingers, so have the tweezers nearby, use them when you need them, and do not let the stickers become a big irritation, physically or psychologically. Like the pads, the fruits have both spines and glochids.

Cactus expert David Eppele suggests that if you wind up with many small stickers in your hand, coat the affected area with white glue. Wait for it to dry thoroughly, then peel it off. It works on the tiniest stickers better than tweezers.

To clean the fruits, hold them one by one with the tongs, scrub them all over with a stiff vegetable brush, rinsing them frequently in a pan of water, to dislodge as many thorns and glochids as possible.

The preparations for juice, purée, and syrup given here are all more or less interchangeable in recipes. If you have one but another is called for in a recipe, try it anyway, just being aware of the sweetness level. The juice is strained and clear; the purée is thicker with more solids. The syrup is, of course, sweetened. You can also purchase prickly pear nectar in some stores

Arizona Cactus Ranch Prickly Pear Nectar is produced without added sugar.

and by mail order (see Sources) from Arizona Cactus Ranch. This unsweetened prickly pear juice includes some solids from Engelmann prickly pears. Because the purée has no preservatives, many people freeze it in smaller containers once they have opened the bottle. It too can be substituted in most of the recipes in this book. If the recipe calls for syrup, you'll have to adjust for sweetness by adding sugar or non-nutritive sweetener. Syrup has enough sugar that it can be stored refrigerated.

PREPARING PRICKLY PEAR FRUIT PIECES Fill a medium-sized saucepan with water and bring to a boil over high heat. Plunge 6 pears into the boiling water and cook from 10 to 20 seconds. Lift them out with a slotted spoon and transfer to a colander. Spear each pear with a long-tined cooking fork, or hold with tongs and peel with a sharp knife. The stickers are softer when hot. Slit each fruit in half and carefully scoop out the seeds with a spoon.

Alternately, you can freeze the prickly pears. As they begin to defrost, the skins will slip off easily. Eight to ten prickly pears will yield 1 cup of fruit chunks.

PRICKLY PEAR PURÉE Follow steps for prickly pear pieces above. Mash with a fork or lightly blend. If you blend too much, the cell walls will break down and you'll have juice.

PRICKLY PEAR JUICE Cut prickly pears into walnut-sized chunks and put 2 to 3 cups of pieces in a blender jar with $1/2$ cup of water, cover, and blend until smooth. Line a strainer with several thicknesses of cheesecloth and strain. If you make more of this than you can use immediately, freeze in plastic containers.

MAKES ABOUT 1 PINT

Prickly Pear Syrup

12 medium prickly pears
Juice of 1 lemon
1½ cups sugar
1 teaspoon cornstarch (optional)

Prickly pear syrup is good on ice cream or pancakes and also appears in a number of recipes in this book. If the fruits you use are particularly large, you'll need a few less; should they be small, you'll need a few more.

Put prickly pears in a bowl or dishpan full of water. Holding each one with tongs, scrub with a vegetable brush to remove dust and some of the stickers (the rest will come out later when you strain the juice). Transfer 6 at a time to a blender jar and process until liquid. Line a mesh strainer with cheesecloth and strain juice into a medium saucepan. You should have about 1 cup. Add lemon juice and sugar, and slowly bring to a simmer. Cook until syrup begins to thicken. If you want a thicker syrup, stir in 1 teaspoon cornstarch dissolved in a little cold water and cook to thicken. Stir with wire whisk if necessary to smooth consistency. (Adding dry cornstarch to hot liquid will result in lumps.)

VARIATION To add depth of flavor to your syrup, eliminate the lemon and instead add 1 small bunch of chopped mint, 1 whole cinnamon stick, and 1 vanilla bean, split lengthwise, and simmer for 20 minutes. Strain out solids before adding cornstarch-and-water mixture.

FOR DIABETICS Use an amount of your favorite non-nutritive sweetener equivalent to 1½ cups of sugar. Since sugar causes thickening, you'll have to compensate by using a little more cornstarch, or use another thickener such as guar gum or xanthan gum, both available at health-food stores.

Santa Rita prickly pear (Opuntia santa-rita) *in the foothills of the Santa Rita Mountains, Arizona.*

A LITTLE BIT ABOUT CHILES Dozens of varieties of chiles grow on our planet, but the recipes in this book use only five of them. However, if you know your chiles, feel free to substitute your favorites in any of the dishes. The relative spiciness of chiles is determined by their rating on the Scoville scale, with zero for the mildest bell peppers and 100,000 for the hotter-than-hot *habañeros*. Chiles are also rated on a "heat scale" of one to ten. Individual chiles within varieties vary in hotness as well, so it's good to

take a tiny little taste before adding the full complement to a recipe. Here are the ones we used, progressing from the mildest to the hottest:

NEW MEXICAN OR ANAHEIMS These are the chiles most often found in cans, called simply "green chiles." When they ripen and turn red, they may be strung on *ristras* or ground into chili powder. They generally reach from six to seven inches long. Their Scoville score ranges from 500 to 2,500, and they rate a two to four on the heat scale.

POBLANOS Originally from the valley of Puebla in Mexico, poblano chiles are called *ancho* chiles when dried. They become very dark, and the pod is a flat heart shape. They are from three to six inches in length. They range from 1,000 to 1,500 on the Scoville scale, rating a three on the heat scale.

JALAPEÑOS These little green chiles vary from three to four inches long and are named for the town of Jalapa, Mexico, where they were first marketed. Their heat-scale level is six and their Scoville score ranges from 2,500 to 5,000.

CHIPOTLES Available dried and canned in sauce, chipotles are jalapeños that have been allowed to ripen to red, then dried and smoked over mesquite wood. Their heat-scale levels and Scoville scores are the same as for unsmoked jalapeños, but the *adobo* sauce they often come in picks up the heat, so use them sparingly.

Prickly pear pads (shown whole at top center, and chopped and bagged below that) and peppers are natural culinary companions and are frequently displayed together in supermarkets. Also shown here: green and red bell peppers on the left, tiny jalapeños in the lower left, and medium-hot, yellow Güero chiles on the right.

SERRANOS Their name is an adjective meaning "from the mountain" because they were first grown in the mountains of northern Puebla and Hidalgo, Mexico. They are thin and range from one to four inches long. They rate 10,000 to 23,000 Scoville units and a six to seven on the heat scale.

BEVERAGES

ARIZONA SUNSETS

PRICKLY PEAR MARGARITAS

PRICKLY PEAR
GRAPEFRUIT MIMOSA

SOMBRERO

CACTUS WINE COOLER

PRICKLY PEAR WINE

EL JEFE'S CACTUS WINE

PRICKLY PEAR LEMONADE

PRICKLY PEAR PUNCH

PRICKLY PEAR SMOOTHIES

Arizona Sunsets

MAKES 4 SERVINGS

1 quart orange juice
½ cup tequila or rum
½ cup prickly pear syrup, commercial or homemade (page 30)
4 slices fresh orange

Be sure to follow the instructions and combine the ingredients in the order listed to get the full effect of these beautiful drinks.

Fill four tall clear glasses with ice. Fill each three-quarters full of orange juice. Divide liquor among glasses (about 1 shot-glass each) and stir. Add 2 tablespoons prickly pear syrup to each glass (it will sink to the bottom). Do not stir. Cut each orange slice halfway through and hang one on rim of each glass.

Prickly Pear Margaritas

MAKES 4 SERVINGS

6 ounces Jose Cuervo Gold tequila
4 ounces Triple Sec
4 ounces lime juice
2 ounces prickly pear syrup, commercial or homemade (page 30)
1 ounce orange juice

Renowned cooking teacher Donna Nordin came to Tucson to give a class in 1983, fell in love with and married the cooking-school owner, Don Luria, and together they opened Café Terra Cotta in 1986. Nordin soon became a major influence in contemporary Southwestern cuisine, and only seven years after Café Terra Cotta opened, Conde Nast Traveler *named it one of America's fifty best restaurants. Café Terra Cotta was one of the first places to serve the prickly pear margarita, now ubiquitous from coast to coast and border to border.*

TO SERVE ON THE ROCKS Mix ingredients and pour over ice into four glasses.

TO SERVE BLENDED Combine ingredients with 4 cups of ice in a blender container and process. Pour into glasses.

Prickly Pear Grapefruit Mimosa

1½ ounces fresh grapefruit juice

1 ounce prickly pear syrup, commercial or homemade (page 30)

3 ounces Champagne

Chris Pedersen, executive sous chef at Westward Look Resort in Tucson, often makes these drinks with fresh grapefruit juice from the many citrus trees on the resort property. He and some of the kitchen staff will each get a bucket and make the rounds of the eighty acres until they each have a bulging load of juicy fruit. Pedersen is an old hand at this. As a youngster he lived near Westward Look, and he and his buddies often would sneak onto the property to "liberate" some of the oranges and grapefruits.

Combine chilled grapefruit juice and prickly pear syrup in Champagne flute. Top with Champagne.

Sombrero

½ cup pineapple juice

1½ ounces rum

½ ounce Triple Sec

½ cup crushed ice

1 ounce prickly pear syrup, nectar, or juice, commercial or homemade (pages 29–30)

1 chunk fresh pineapple

Although prickly pear syrup is sweetened and prickly pear nectar and juice are not, this drink recipe works well with whichever product you have on hand. If you use syrup, the pink and fruity drink will come out a little sweeter than if you use juice or nectar.

Combine juice, rum, Triple Sec, and ice, and blend at high speed. Pour into a glass and top with prickly pear syrup or nectar. Serve with a swizzle stick speared onto a chunk of pineapple.

Cactus Wine Cooler

1 scoop crushed ice

1 tablespoon prickly pear syrup,
commercial or homemade (page 30)

½ glass Chablis wine

½ glass 7-Up

The Cactus Wine Cooler is a popular drink at El Corral in Tucson—a comfortable restaurant locally famous for its prime rib and steaks.

Combine all ingredients in a glass and shake well.

Prickly Pear Wine

4 pounds dark-red prickly pears

4 oranges

4 lemons

4 quarts boiling water

4 pounds sugar

1 yeast cake

1 slice toasted white bread

I have not tried this recipe, which comes from Kooking with Kaktus, *published by the Houston Cactus and Succulent Society many years ago. I offer it to those who already make wine and know what they are doing.*

Cut up prickly pears, oranges, and lemons, and put in large crock. Pour boiling water over mixture; cover and let stand 4 days. Scoop out fruit, mash, and strain into bowl through colander lined with cheesecloth. Strain liquid through cheesecloth a second time. Discard solids. Wash crock and return all liquid. Add sugar and stir to dissolve. Dissolve yeast cake in ¼ cup water and soak toasted bread in yeast mixture. Float toast on top of fruit juice and cover. Allow to stand 4 days. Remove toast.

Put fermenting liquid into a large bottle with a cork stopper fitted with a piece of glass tube to which can be attached a hose of sufficient length to submerge in a container of clear water. As long as fermentation continues, bubbles will percolate from the end of the hose. When bubbles no longer appear, fermentation is complete. Bottle, seal tightly, and allow to stand 4 months in a cool, dark place.

El Jefe's Cactus Wine

MAKES ABOUT 5 QUARTS

2-gallon bucket of prickly pears
2 quarts of water

The late David Eppele kept in touch with cactus lovers all over the world through his organization, Arizona Cactus and Succulent Research. Every Labor Day he threw a big fiesta at his Cactus and Succulent Research Center in Bisbee, Arizona. All were invited and plied with El Jefe's (Eppele's) homemade prickly pear wine. It had become an annual tradition, and his guests looked forward to toasting the end of the hot summer with the sweet libation. Honesty compels me to admit I have neither made nor tasted this wine, but El Jefe promised he never killed anybody. While the juice is fermenting it may smell pungent, but do not cover with screw-down caps, or the jars will explode.

This recipe may be expanded to use as much prickly pear juice as you have.

1 gallon fresh prickly pear juice
(as described above)
5 cups sugar
2 packages yeast

Wash prickly pears in a two-gallon bucket, using a garden hose and letting the water spill onto a plant that needs a drink. Dump the fruits into a large kettle and add water. Bring to a boil. When the fruits are soft, drain them in a colander. Set the colander over a bowl and mash the fruit with a potato masher. Strain juice through three layers of cheesecloth. Measure juice and proceed with following recipe:

Mix all the ingredients in a non-reactive container such as a pottery crock or one-gallon glass jar. Cover with a clean cloth and place in a cool dark place for 4 weeks. Strain, chill, and serve.

MAKES 4 SERVINGS

Prickly Pear Lemonade

4 or 5 lemons

6 cups water

¼ to ½ cup sugar (or equivalent
non-nutritive sweetener)

¼ cup prickly pear juice or syrup
(pages 29 and 30)

Ice

Steeping the lemons rather than squeezing them is not only easier, it produces a more complex flavor as the final juice includes lemon oil from the rind.

Scrub lemons and slice ¼-inch thick. Place in a large heat-proof bowl or pitcher. Bring water to a boil and pour over lemons. Stir in sugar. (Use less if you'll be adding prickly pear syrup, more if you'll use juice.) Let sit for 4 hours. Strain off juice and add prickly pear product. Taste and correct for sweetness. Refrigerate or serve immediately over ice.

MAKES ABOUT 20 SERVINGS

Prickly Pear Punch

6-ounce can frozen orange-juice
concentrate, thawed

1½ cups prickly pear juice (page 29)

1½ cups pineapple juice

¼ cup freshly squeezed lemon juice

28-ounce bottle of ginger ale

Ice ring frozen with fruits and
mint for color

Every year near the beginning of school, the University of Arizona Faculty Women's Club holds a Newcomers Coffee. Many of the women attending the event are new to the desert as well as to the university. To acquaint them with their natural surroundings, the established members traditionally serve Prickly Pear Punch. This means that the second vice president needs to think ahead and harvest the fruits in the summer and store them in her freezer until the October event. In their cookbook Prickly Pear Punch and Other Recipes, *the members write, "We feel that in order to provide a wonder year for FWC, keep the stock market rising and the U of A winning basketball games…the famous Prickly Pear Punch is a necessity."*

Mix fruit juices in punch bowl. Just before serving, add the ginger ale and ice ring.

MAKES 2 SERVINGS

Prickly Pear Smoothies

½ cup prickly pear juice or purée (page 29)

1 cup plain or vanilla yogurt

½ cup orange or pineapple juice

1 cup fresh fruit pieces (combination of cantaloupe, watermelon, peach slices, strawberries, bananas)

2 ice cubes

1 tablespoon honey or other sweetener

You can adjust the ingredients for this smoothie to what you have on hand that is fresh. In the winter, use bottled juice or home-frozen juice or purée, frozen fruit, and bananas.

Combine all ingredients in blender jar and whirl until combined. Taste and adjust sweetener if desired.

APPETIZERS

CEVICHE CON TUNA

EASY NOPALITO SALSA

WIL'S PRICKLY PEAR SALSA

FUNDIDO DE NOPALITO
(NOPALITO FONDUE)

OPERA HOUSE MEATBALLS

VICTORIA'S
FRENCH-FRIED CACTUS

MAKES 4 SERVINGS

Ceviche con Tuna

Rosa Mexicano was one of the first restaurants to bring upscale Mexican food to New York City and has been named Best Mexican Restaurant by New York *magazine year after year. This recipe was developed by the restaurant's culinary director, Roberto Santibañez.*

Born in Mexico City, Santibañez formerly cooked and studied in Paris and owned three restaurants in downtown Mexico City. "Tuna" is the term used for the prickly pear fruit in Mexico, and this recipe calls for juice from the pale green variety as those are more frequently imported to New York. The acid in the lime juice "cooks" the fish, turning the flesh opaque.

TO MAKE THE CEVICHE

1 pound mahimahi fillets, skin and bones removed

1 cup lime juice (approximately 8 to 10 limes, depending on size)

Salt

FOR THE MARINADE

1½ cups prickly pear juice

½ fresh poblano chile pepper, chopped

2 small tomatillos (fresh), chopped

2 scallions (green parts only), finely sliced

¼ small red onion, finely chopped

2 tablespoons chopped cilantro (generous)

2 tablespoons simple syrup (directions follow)

1½ tablespoons olive oil (does not need to be extra-virgin)

Cut the fish in ¼-inch-square pieces, transfer to a colander, and wash lightly under running water. Transfer to a small bowl and cover with the lime juice. It is important that the lime juice completely cover the fish. Season with salt.

Let sit in the refrigerator for at least 30 minutes but no longer than 1 hour or it will overcook.

Meanwhile, combine the marinade ingredients in a medium bowl. Remove fish from refrigerator and strain and reserve the juice. Measure ½ cup and add it and fish to the marinade. Refrigerate for 1 hour. Serve in chilled martini glasses.

To make simple syrup: Mix 1½ tablespoons water with ½ tablespoon sugar. Bring to a boil, stir until clear, then cool. You may mix equivalent non-nutritive sweetener with water to substitute for the sugar.

Easy Nopalito Salsa

MAKES ABOUT 1½ CUPS

½ cup prepared salsa

½ cup canned black beans

½ cup cleaned, cooked, and diced fresh prickly pear pads (pages 26–27) or canned nopalitos

1 tablespoon chopped fresh cilantro

1 tablespoon fresh lime juice

Starting with your favorite commercial salsa and canned beans lets you put this dish together in a hurry. Serve this salsa with chips or as a topping for chicken, fish, or grilled steak.

If you use canned nopalitos, rinse them several times in a wire strainer, then chop. Combine all ingredients in a medium bowl.

Wil's Prickly Pear Salsa

MAKES A GENEROUS QUART

2 cups prickly pear fruit pieces (page 29)

2 cups sugar

1–2 tablespoons each, minced red and green jalapeños

½ cup chopped onion

Juice of ½ lime

Zest of 1 lime

¼ cup diced nopalitos (1/4 inch)

¼ cup strongly flavored tequila (optional)

2 tablespoons chopped cilantro leaves

Cayenne pepper to taste

This recipe was developed by Wil Power, chef at the historic Washington Hotel in the friendly little town of Washington in the Gold Rush country north of Sacramento, California. The hotel, on the banks of the blue green South Yuba River, once played host to the likes of Wyatt and Josephine Earp and President Grover Cleveland. Reduce the quantity of jalapeños for a milder salsa.

Macerate prickly pear fruit and any accumulated juices in sugar for 1½ to 2 hours. Drain and reserve liquid.

In a medium saucepan, combine reserved liquid, jalapeños, onion, lime juice, and zest. Simmer until onion is clear, then add nopalitos and prickly pear fruit solids. Simmer 10 minutes. If mixture becomes too thick, add up to ¼ cup tequila or water.

MAKES 4 APPETIZER SERVINGS

Fundido de Nopalito (Nopalito Fondue)

¾ cup nopalitos, cut into ¾-inch dice

¼ cup bulk chorizo

6 ounces grated Chihuahua or Monterey Jack cheese

Chef Arturo Rodriguez and his brother Jorge own the charming Phoenix restaurant Asi Es La Vida (Such Is Life). This recipe was a winner in 1992 in the Phoenix New Times alternative weekly newspaper "Best of Phoenix" survey. *Chihuahua cheese is a white cow's-milk cheese frequently used in Mexican cooking. Also known as* asadero, *it becomes soft and stringy when melted. Chorizo is a Mexican sausage, highly seasoned with garlic and chile. This recipe may be easily doubled or quadrupled.*

Prepare nopalitos following your choice of directions on pages 26–27. In a frying pan over medium heat, stir and cook chorizo until done. Drain fat. Add nopalitos and combine. Transfer to ovenproof casserole or pan. Top with cheese and heat in preheated 400-degree oven until cheese melts. Serve with tortilla chips or fresh warm corn or flour tortillas and salsa.

MAKES 32 SMALL MEATBALLS (OR
4 TO 6 MAIN-DISH SERVINGS)

1 pound ground beef

1 egg, beaten

¾ cup bread crumbs

¼ cup finely chopped red onion

¼ teaspoon salt

Southwest Sauce (recipe follows)

½ cup prickly pear syrup, commercial
or homemade (page 30)

½ cup water

¼ cup molasses

2 tablespoons tomato paste

2 tablespoons white vinegar

2 teaspoons salt

½ teaspoon flour

Dash of mustard

Dash of garlic powder

Dash of red chile powder

Opera House Meatballs

Chef Matthew Vimmerstedt developed these meatballs for parties at the Savoy Opera House, a catering hall for private parties in Trail Dust Town, a Wild West-themed shopping and dining destination in Tucson. The Opera House is decorated in 1800s style. Serve the meatballs with toothpicks.

Preheat oven to 350 degrees. In medium bowl, combine all ingredients except sauce, mixing lightly with your hands. Form into 32 balls approximately ½ inch in diameter (make 1-inch balls if you want to serve them as a main dish). Arrange on rimmed cookie sheet and bake for about 20 minutes. Meanwhile, make sauce. When meatballs and sauce are both done, transfer meatballs to shallow casserole, cover with Southwest Sauce, and bake uncovered for 10 minutes. Serve hot.

SOUTHWEST SAUCE   Combine ingredients in medium saucepan. Cook over medium heat, stirring constantly until sauce bubbles and begins to thicken.

Victoria's French-Fried Cactus

MAKES 4 SERVINGS

2 prickly pear pads, cleaned (page 25)

1 egg

³/₄ cup cornmeal

Salt and pepper

Cumin (optional)

¹/₂ cup vegetable oil (or enough to cover bottom of frying pan at least ¹/₄ inch deep)

Do you really like nopalitos? Here's a recipe for the purist from Victoria and John Dicus, who grow organic prickly pear cactus in Nipomo, California. Through their company, Rivenrock Gardens, they sell several varieties of cactus pads and ship them to happy customers all over the country. John's favorite recipe is fried cactus strips. The Dicuses use the nearly spineless Nopal Grande, a variety from Mexico's Yucatan Peninsula that has been cultivated there for centuries. They pick the pads when they are about 6 to 8 inches long.

These are delicious when served with a spicy salsa dip or barbecue sauce. I stirred a couple of tablespoons of Zeman's Prickly Pear Barbecue Sauce (see page 116 for ordering information) into a mixture of mayonnaise and plain yogurt, and it made a great complement to the crispy strips.

Cut cleaned cactus pads into strips about ³/₈-inch wide. Crack egg into a small bowl and beat with a fork until frothy. Put cornmeal in a shallow bowl and season with salt, pepper, and cumin if desired. Heat oil in a large frying pan. Dip cactus strips in egg, then roll in cornmeal and place into the hot oil. Turn to brown both sides. When coating is crisp, lift from oil with tongs. Drain on paper towels. Serve immediately with a flavorful sauce.

SALADS AND DRESSINGS

GAZPACHO ASPIC

JICAMA NOPALITO SALAD

ROMAINE AND NOPALITO SALAD
WITH ORANGES AND QUESO BLANCO

CLASSIC MEXICAN NOPALITO SALAD

SWEET MIRIN PRICKLY
PEAR VINAIGRETTE

PRICKLY PEAR LIME DRESSING

1 to 2 cleaned prickly pear pads to yield ½ cup chopped nopalitos

1 envelope unflavored gelatin

1 cup tomato juice

½ cup finely diced tomatoes

½ cup peeled, finely chopped cucumber

½ cup finely chopped green bell pepper

¼ cup finely sliced green onion

1 clove garlic, minced or pressed

2 tablespoons olive oil

¼ cup red-wine vinegar

Hot-pepper seasoning to taste

6 to 8 large lettuce leaves

Gazpacho Aspic

This excellent hot-weather dish is good served alongside a quiche or sandwich for lunch. Waiting until the tomato juice and gelatin mixture has thickened a little before adding the vegetables helps keep them evenly suspended.

Cook prickly pear pads lightly, following directions of your choice on pages 26–27. Mince and set aside. In a small pan, sprinkle gelatin over tomato juice. Let soften for 5 minutes, then place over medium heat and stir until gelatin is dissolved. Let cool to room temperature. Refrigerate until gelatin mixture becomes syrupy.

Meanwhile, peel, seed, and finely chop tomatoes. Stir tomatoes into the cooled gelatin mixture with the nopalitos, cucumber, bell pepper, onion, garlic, oil, vinegar, and hot-pepper seasoning. With cold water, rinse a mold that holds at least 4 cups. Pour mixture into mold and refrigerate until firm, about 4 hours.

To serve, line plate with lettuce leaves. Invert mold onto greens. Soak a towel in hot water and wring out. Cover mold with hot towel until gelatin releases from mold and settles onto greens.

MAKES 8 TO 10 SERVINGS

Jicama Nopalito Salad

2½ cups nopalitos (cleaned and chopped prickly pear pads, pages 26–27), chopped into ³⁄₈ -inch dice

½ pound of jicama, peeled and chopped into ³⁄₈ -inch dice

2 red jalapeño chiles, chopped into confetti dice

1 yellow bell pepper, chopped into ³⁄₈ -inch dice

1 European cucumber, peeled, seeded, and chopped into ³⁄₈ -inch dice

¼ cup chives, chopped

¼ cup fresh mint leaves picked from stems

¼ cup cilantro leaves, picked from stems

Sweet Mirin Prickly Pear Vinaigrette (page 59)

4 cups purslane or mixed greens, washed

The chefs at Westward Look Resort in Tucson have a reputation for including local produce in the Southwest-inspired foods they prepare. A garden on the property provides some of the ingredients. Chef Chris Pedersen, a Tucson native, gathers purslane for this salad after the summer "monsoon" rains. Purslane grows world-wide in disturbed soil. Most Americans consider it a weed, but it is eaten in many cultures (Spanish speakers call it verdolaga*). Recent studies show it is high in healthful omega-3 fatty acids.*

Bring two small pots of water to a boil. Place the cleaned, diced nopalitos into one pot for 30 to 45 seconds, or until the water begins to thicken. Drain and transfer immediately to the second pot for another 30 to 45 seconds. Do not overcook. Drain well.

In a medium bowl, combine nopalitos with jicama, jalapeños, bell pepper, cucumber, and chives. Using a very sharp knife, cut mint and cilantro leaves into fine shreds. Stir into nopalitos and jicama mixture. Toss with vinaigrette and marinate in refrigerator until ready to serve. Mound on a bed of fresh purslane or greens.

Romaine and Nopalito Salad with Oranges and Queso Blanco (See photo on page 18)

MAKES 4 SERVINGS

2 small prickly pear pads, cleaned (page 25)
1 teaspoon olive oil
2 large oranges
4 green onions, sliced
1 cup diced, drained fresh tomatoes
1/4 to 1/2 cup coarsely chopped cilantro
Anise Vinaigrette (recipe follows)
16 leaves of romaine lettuce from center of head
1/4 cup crumbled queso blanco

Before Janos Wilder even opened his popular Janos Restaurant in Tucson in 1983, he was looking for sources of top-quality local produce—especially those products that evoke the Southwest's culinary traditions. This salad typifies the original and delicious combinations of ingredients one expects when eating at Janos. Queso blanco *is a crumbly white unaged cheese available in Mexican grocery stores. You can substitute mild feta cheese if queso blanco is not available.*

Brush the prickly pear pads on both sides lightly with olive oil. Broil, grill, or cook in large frying pan until they brown a little bit but are not too soft. Slice them into thin strips (to make nopalitos) and set aside. With a very sharp knife, cut peel from oranges, removing all the white material. Working over a bowl, cut orange segments from between the membranes.

Toss nopalitos, orange sections, green onion, tomatoes, and cilantro with a little of the Anise Vinaigrette. Toss the romaine leaves lightly in the dressing. To arrange individual salads, mound romaine toward one side of each salad plate. Heap the nopalito mixture at the base of the leaves. Sprinkle each serving with the queso blanco.

MAKES 2 CUPS

4 star-anise pods
1 1/3 cups olive oil
2/3 cup Sherry vinegar
3 tablespoons dry tarragon
3 tablespoons chopped shallot
Salt and pepper

ANISE VINAIGRETTE Pound star anise to break into several pieces. Combine ingredients in medium bowl and let steep for a couple of hours. Remove star-anise pieces, then whisk until creamy and well combined.

MAKES 2 SERVINGS

Classic Mexican Nopalito Salad

2 medium nopales (cactus pads), cleaned (page 25)

1 tablespoon vegetable oil

½ cup finely chopped tomatoes

2 tablespoons finely minced onion

1 teaspoon finely minced garlic

1 tablespoon chopped green chiles, canned or fresh

1 or 2 finely minced serrano chiles

2 tablespoons chopped cilantro

1 tablespoon lime juice

2 tablespoons finely crumbled queso blanco, queso fresco, or feta cheese

This classic Mexican cactus salad comes in as many different versions as American potato salad. Here is the way I like it best, with the nopalitos chopped very fine. This recipe makes just two servings, a good sample if you are making it for the first time. I suspect that the second time you make it you will want to double or triple the recipe. Chef Ed Lake frequently made a version of this recipe when he was in charge of one of the dining rooms at the United Nations.

Heat oven to 375 degrees. Cut nopales in strips about 1 inch wide. Brush on both sides with vegetable oil and arrange on a cookie sheet. Roast for 10 minutes or until they have become olive green, then turn pieces over to cook the other sides. When cool, slice each strip into pieces the width of a wooden matchstick and half as long. Combine in a medium bowl along with remaining ingredients. Stir to combine. Refrigerate until ready to serve on lettuce leaves or as a stuffing for hot-off-the-griddle corn tortillas.

PUEBLA STYLE Substitute cooked green beans for half the nopales. Use minced fresh oregano instead of cilantro and grated mozzarella for the cheese.

TOLUCA STYLE Add finely minced fresh radishes.

Sweet Mirin Prickly Pear Vinaigrette

MAKES ABOUT 3 CUPS

½ cup sugar

1 cup sweet mirin saki (rice wine)

1 cup prickly pear syrup, commercial or homemade (page 30)

1 tablespoon fresh-ground black pepper

1 tablespoon kosher salt

1 lime, juiced

2 tablespoons olive oil

2 tablespoons white balsamic vinegar

The elegant Sunday brunches at the Westward Look Resort in Tucson are legendary. The offerings vary, but this salad dressing appears frequently.

In a small saucepan, combine the sugar and mirin saki to make a simple syrup and reduce by half. Remove from heat and add all other ingredients, mixing well. Chill.

Prickly Pear Lime Dressing

MAKES ABOUT 3 CUPS

Juice and zest of 2 limes

½ cup prickly pear syrup, commercial or homemade (page 30)

¼ cup raspberry vinegar

1 tablespoon balsamic vinegar

1 tablespoon red-wine vinegar

1 cup canola oil

¼ cup olive oil

¼ cup light corn syrup

½ jalapeño, finely diced

6 basil leaves, finely julienned

Another Westward Look Resort favorite, this is especially good on a salad incorporating both greens and fruits.

In a small mixing bowl, add all ingredients. Mix well. Season to taste with kosher salt and fresh-ground black pepper.

BAKED GOODS, PRESERVES, AND SAUCES

GALLETAS DE NOPALITO

NOPALITO MUFFINS

PRICKLY PEAR KUCHEN

PRICKLY PEAR MUFFINS

CHERI'S ARIZONA
SUNRISE MUFFINS

CACTUS DATE CONSERVE

PRICKLY PEAR AND APPLE BUTTER

PRICKLY PEAR COMPOTE

ROSY ONION JAM

PRICKLY PEAR JELLY

NATALIE'S PRICKLY
PEAR BARBECUE SAUCE

MAKES 18 BISCUITS

Galletas de Nopalito

**1 cup grated prickly pear cactus pad
(about 2 medium-sized pads)**

1 egg, beaten

2 tablespoons vegetable oil

2 tablespoons finely sliced green onion

**1 tablespoon finely minced jalapeño or
green Anaheim chiles**

1 cup all-purpose flour

1 teaspoon baking powder

¹⁄₂ teaspoon salt

¹⁄₂ cup grated cheese of your choice

These biscuits make a great accompaniment to soup or salad. Don't be put off by the viscosity of the grated-cactus-and-egg mixture. It disappears when the biscuits are baked. If you are very sensitive to anything spicy, use Anaheim chiles instead of jalapeños, or omit the chiles entirely.

Preheat oven to 400 degrees. Place grated prickly pear pads in a medium bowl. Add beaten egg, oil, onion, and chiles, and combine. Stir in dry ingredients. Finally, stir in grated cheese. Drop by rounded tablespoons onto greased baking sheet. Bake 20 minutes or until bottoms and tops are lightly browned. Serve immediately.

MAKES 12 LARGE MUFFINS
OR 18 SMALLER ONES

Nopalito Muffins

1 cup finely chopped prickly
pear pads (page 25)

$^1\!/_2$ cup finely chopped onions

$^1\!/_2$ cup finely chopped red bell pepper

$^1\!/_4$ cup finely chopped green bell pepper

2 tablespoons finely chopped
jalapeño chiles

1 tablespoon vegetable oil

1 cup yellow cornmeal

$1^1\!/_2$ cups flour

3 tablespoons brown sugar (or
equivalent non-nutritive sweetener)

$2^1\!/_2$ teaspoons baking powder

1 teaspoon black pepper

$^1\!/_2$ teaspoon salt

1 egg

$^1\!/_4$ cup vegetable oil

$1^1\!/_2$ cups milk

1 cup grated Monterey Jack cheese

Cleo Kraatz, a baker in Riviera, Texas, won a first-place ribbon in the 1996 Texas Cactus Cook-off for these hearty muffins.

Preheat oven to 400 degrees. In a large frying pan, sauté vegetables (including prickly pear pieces) in vegetable oil until tender. Set aside. In a large bowl, combine the dry ingredients. In another bowl, beat the egg. Add the remaining wet ingredients, including cheese, and combine. Stir in the sautéed vegetables. Add wet ingredients to dry ingredients and stir to combine.

Fill greased muffin cups two-thirds full. Bake for 15 to 20 minutes or until lightly browned.

MAKES A 9 X 12-INCH CAKE

Prickly Pear Kuchen

1 cup white flour

1 cup whole wheat flour

½ teaspoon baking powder

½ teaspoon salt

1 cup brown sugar

½ cup butter

2 cups prickly pear fruit halves (page 29)

1 teaspoon cinnamon

½ teaspoon nutmeg

1 cup sour cream

2 eggs, beaten

1 teaspoon vanilla

1 teaspoon orange juice

1 teaspoon grated orange rind

This makes an excellent brunch dish, rich and fruity but not too sweet.

Preheat oven to 400 degrees. Combine the flours, baking powder, salt, and 2 tablespoons of the sugar in a large bowl. Cut in the butter with a pastry blender or transfer to food-processor bowl and process with the steel blade until the mixture looks like coarse meal. Press mixture firmly into a 9 x 12-inch baking pan. Arrange halved prickly pears on the surface of the crust. Mix spices and remaining sugar and sprinkle over the fruit. Bake 15 minutes.

Meanwhile, in a medium bowl combine the sour cream, eggs, vanilla, orange juice, and orange rind. Once baking is finished, remove pan from oven and spread mixture evenly over cake. Reduce oven temperature to 375 degrees and bake 30 minutes longer. Cool before serving.

2 cups flour

2 teaspoons baking powder

¼ cup sugar

½ teaspoon cinnamon

1/4 teaspoon salt

1 egg

½ cup milk

¼ cup oil

1 cup prickly pear fruit pieces
(page 29)

Prickly Pear Muffins   (See photo on page 60, top right)

Before you stir in the prickly pear pieces, look them over carefully to make sure you have removed every last seed. Biting down on a stone-like seed in a soft muffin can make for a jarring experience.

Preheat oven to 400 degrees. Sift the dry ingredients together into a mixing bowl. In a separate bowl, beat the egg; add the milk and oil and combine. Add the wet ingredients to the dry ingredients, stirring only enough to moisten the flour. Gently stir in the prickly pear pieces and any juice that has accumulated in the container.

Spoon the batter into greased muffin tins, filling them about two-thirds full. Bake the muffins for 20 minutes or until golden brown.

MAKES 12 LARGE MUFFINS
OR 18 SMALLER ONES

2 cups all-purpose flour

¼ cup sugar

3 teaspoons baking powder

½ teaspoon salt

¼ cup vegetable oil

1 egg, slightly beaten

1 cup milk

¼ cup prickly pear jelly
(see page 72)

Cheri's Arizona Sunrise Muffins

Cheri Romanowski began making cactus jelly at home and now has a company called Cheri's Desert Harvest that produces jelly, syrup, and candies from prickly pear fruit. Her syrup sells nationwide by the palletful to restaurants for use in prickly pear margaritas. Cheri is a very hands-on company owner, frequently found in her factory's kitchen stirring a big vat of deep-magenta juice. She developed the following recipe using her Cheri's Desert Harvest Prickly Pear Jelly.

Preheat oven to 400 degrees. Sift flour, sugar, baking powder, and salt together and set aside. Mix oil, egg, and milk and add to dry ingredients. Stir until moistened. Batter will be lumpy. Fill greased muffin tins half full. Place 1 teaspoon of jelly in the exact center of each muffin, with jelly not touching edges. Add remaining batter, covering jelly, so that tins are two-thirds full. Bake for 20 to 25 minutes or until golden brown.

MAKES 5 TO 6 MEDIUM JARS

Cactus Date Conserve

1 orange

2 cups thinly sliced prickly pear fruit (page 29)

18 dates, chopped and pitted

1/2 cup canned pineapple bits, drained

4 teaspoons lemon juice

1/2 cup pineapple juice

1 1/2 cups sugar

1/3 cup broken walnut meats

Jars of this conserve make excellent Christmas or hostess gifts. You can clean the fruit and freeze it when it ripens during the late summer or early fall, then cook up the conserve when you have time.

Grate orange rind and squeeze the juice into a medium saucepan with a heavy bottom. Add remaining ingredients except nutmeats and stir to combine. Cook slowly over medium-low heat until close to desired jamlike consistency. Add the nutmeats and cook for about 5 more minutes. Pack in sterile jars and refrigerate or process in hot-water bath to seal.

MAKES ABOUT 2 CUPS

Prickly Pear and Apple Butter

2 apples

1 large orange, to yield 1/2 cup juice and 1 tablespoon grated peel

1 cup prickly pear fruit pieces (page 29)

This simple-to-make treat is good on toast or as a topping for broiled fish such as salmon.

Core and chop unpeeled apples into 1/2-inch dice. Combine apples and orange juice in a medium saucepan with a heavy bottom. Bring to a simmer over medium heat, then turn heat down so ingredients barely simmer. Cook 15–20 minutes until apples are tender. Transfer apples to blender container and whirl until smooth. Add prickly pear pieces and blend briefly. Return to pot and stir in grated orange peel. Cook carefully to desired thickness. Transfer to freshly washed jars. Refrigerate.

MAKES 2 CUPS

Prickly Pear Compote

Clarified butter for sautéing

1 yellow onion, chopped into medium dice

2 Anaheim chiles, peeled, seeded, and chopped into medium dice

1 teaspoon chopped fresh garlic

3 tablespoons julienned dried tomatoes

¼ cup diced red bell peppers

3 tablespoons cooked black beans

Salt and freshly ground pepper to taste

1 cup prickly pear juice (page 29)

3 tablespoons fresh lime juice

1 cup veal stock or beef stock

¼ cup raw sweet corn kernels

Janos Wilder, chef-owner of Janos Restaurant and the less formal J Bar, is a trend-setter in Southwestern cuisine. A consistent winner of culinary awards, he was named Top Chef in the Southwest by the James Beard Foundation in 2000. Wilder marries French cooking techniques with indigenous ingredients from the Southwest to create dishes as delicious as they are beautiful.

In a large sauté pan, heat enough clarified butter to coat pan, and sauté onion until almost translucent. Add the chiles and garlic and sauté 1 minute longer. Add tomatoes, bell peppers, beans, salt, and pepper, and stir vigorously to combine all ingredients.

Add prickly pear juice, lime juice, and stock, and bring to a boil. Reduce to 2 cups, stirring constantly to avoid scorching. In a small sauté pan, heat a little butter, sauté the corn, and add it to the sauce. Refrigerate; will keep for four or five days.

MAKES ABOUT 1 PINT

Rosy Onion Jam

1¼ pounds red onions

¼ cup minced shallots

1 tablespoon minced garlic

2 tablespoons olive oil

1½ tablespoons lightly packed orange zest (1 large or 2 smaller oranges)

¾ cup prickly pear syrup, commercial or homemade (page 30)

¼ cup red-wine vinegar

This goes well with grilled or roasted meat or chicken or vegetarian dishes like vegetable quiche—or try it on a sandwich. The recipe can be easily doubled or tripled. You do need to keep tabs on the cooking process, so plan to make this onion jam when you're going to be in the kitchen doing other activities. A pint jar makes a wonderful gift.

Peel and quarter the onions and slice thinly. Combine with shallots and garlic and add to medium heavy-bottomed saucepan in which you have heated 2 tablespoons of olive oil over medium heat. Stir onions occasionally until sizzling.

Cover the pan and turn down the heat to very low. Let the onions sweat and slowly cook, becoming sweet. Check from time to time, and if they are sticking, add a tablespoon or 2 of water. Cook for about 30 minutes until translucent and slightly brown.

Add orange zest, prickly pear syrup, and red-wine vinegar, and cook, uncovered, until liquid has evaporated. You will need to stir frequently at this stage. Pack in jars. Refrigerate or process in water bath.

Prickly Pear Jelly

1 package powdered pectin
2½ cups prickly pear juice
3 tablespoons lemon or lime juice
3½ cups sugar

This recipe for Prickly Pear Jelly comes from the home economists at the Pima County (Arizona) Extension Service. It usually works, but the making of a firm jelly depends on a number of complicated reactions. Because prickly pears are a wild fruit, the home cook has no way to gauge their exact chemical properties. Cheri Romanowski of Cheri's Desert Harvest ended up having to call in a food chemist to help her devise a foolproof method for making her commercial jelly. You will have the best luck by following this recipe exactly, using several under-ripe pears and adding a little lemon or lime juice for added pectin. If your jelly doesn't set up, call it syrup, and use it in the many delicious recipes in this book calling for prickly pear syrup. This recipe calls for cooking the fruit before juicing, rather than following the directions for raw juice given in "The Basics" section.

TO PREPARE THE FRUIT Using tongs, gather 15 to 20 prickly pears. Choose red, ripe fruits, with a few underripe ones also. Roll them on the ground to get off the large stickers. Fill a bowl or dishpan with water and rinse the fruit, scrubbing lightly with a vegetable brush. Slice each fruit into two or three pieces and transfer to a large pot; barely cover with water. Bring to a boil, then turn the heat down to simmer and cook for 20 to 25 minutes. Mash with a potato masher or process in a blender or food processor. Line a colander or wire strainer with two thicknesses of cheesecloth and strain the juice. Set strained juice aside so sediment can settle to the bottom. For a clear jelly, do not use this sediment. Measure juice; you will need 2½ cups. If you have more than this, boil it down to concentrate. The stronger the juice, the tastier your jelly will be.

TO PREPARE JELLY Combine pectin and juice in a medium saucepan. Stirring constantly, bring to a fast boil and add the lemon or lime juice and sugar. Bring to a hard boil and boil for exactly 3 minutes. Timing is important for getting a good jell. Remove from the heat. Stir and skim off foam. Pour at once into sterilized jelly jars. If necessary, wipe the edges of the jars with a clean, damp cloth. Seal immediately with clean, hot two-part metal lids, screwing the metal band on firmly. Store in a cool, dry place.

Natalie's Prickly Pear Barbecue Sauce

MAKES ABOUT 3½ CUPS

1¼ cups Arizona Cactus Ranch prickly pear nectar (or homemade juice, page 29)

¾ cup unsweetened frozen apple-juice concentrate

½ cup diced green bell peppers

½ cup apple-cider vinegar

½ cup red-chile paste

2 tablespoons fresh or canned diced green chiles

1 tablespoon diced fresh jalapeños

1 envelope unflavored gelatin or ¹⁄₁₆ teaspoon xanthan gum

4 teaspoons soy sauce

Pinch of sea salt

Natalie McGee produces unsweetened prickly pear nectar from the Arizona Cactus Ranch, on her family homestead in Southern Arizona. She counts many diabetics among her customers. Her recipe for barbecue sauce uses frozen apple-juice concentrate instead of sugar for sweetening, but has plenty of kick with three kinds of chiles. Cut down on the chile ingredients if you want a milder sauce. Xanthan gum is a natural vegetarian thickener available in many health-food stores. This sauce will hold for several weeks in the refrigerator.

Combine all ingredients in blender jar and process until smooth. Transfer to a heavy saucepan and simmer 20 minutes or until thick. Use immediately on any type of meat or refrigerate or freeze for later use.

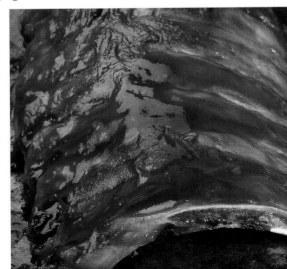

CHICKEN AND CORN CAKES WITH
NOPALITO CHIPOTLE SAUCE

CHICKEN YUCATAN

NOPALES Y POLLO EN PIMIENTO
DULCE ROJO (NOPALES AND
CHICKEN IN RED BELL PEPPER)

GRILLED CHICKEN WITH
NOPALITO AND PINEAPPLE SALSA

CARNE ASADA CON
NOPALES Y TOMATILLO

BEEF WITH PRICKLY PEAR
AND PORT SAUCE

PRICKLY PEAR PORK TENDERLOIN

FISH IN NOPALITO SHRIMP SAUCE

PRICKLY PEAR BARBECUE
SHRIMP WITH ROASTED CORN
AND BLACK BEAN RELISH

NOPAL FRITTATA

NOPALITO RATATOUILLE

SOUTHWESTERN CASSEROLE

PERUVIAN NOPALITO RICE

Chicken and Corn Cakes with Nopalito Chipotle Sauce

MAKES 6 SERVINGS

1 cup raw, cleaned nopalitos chopped into ¼ -inch dice (page 25)

1 tablespoon olive oil, divided

1 medium onion, coarsely chopped

2 cloves garlic, minced

2 tomatoes, chopped

½ to 2 chipotle chiles in adobo sauce

½ cup hulled pumpkin seeds

1 cup chicken broth

½ teaspoon salt

¾ cup flour

½ cup cornmeal

½ teaspoon baking powder

1 teaspoon salt

1 teaspoon sugar (optional)

1 egg

1½ cups buttermilk, divided

3 tablespoons butter, melted, divided

1 cup fresh or frozen corn kernels, divided

1 cup raw, cleaned nopalitos chopped into ¼ -inch dice, divided (page 25)

2 green onions, chopped

Abel Villareal is an occupational therapist in Corpus Christi, Texas, but he loves to cook and spends many of his vacations attending cooking seminars. His training is evident in this dish, which won a blue ribbon in the 1997 Texas Cactus Council cook-off. It is so good, we ate the leftovers for breakfast. Be careful with the chipotle chiles; they are very spicy.

NOPALITO CHIPOTLE PUMPKIN SEED SAUCE In large frying pan over medium heat, sauté nopalitos in ½ teaspoon olive oil until they have turned olive green and are slightly shriveled looking. Add remaining oil, onion, and garlic and sauté 2 to 3 minutes or until onion is translucent. Add chopped tomato and cook another minute or two until soft. Purée chipotle chiles and pumpkin seeds with chicken broth and salt in blender. Add to sauté ingredients and simmer over very low heat for 3 minutes. Set aside and keep warm. (Can be made a day or two ahead and refrigerated.)

NOPALITO CORN CAKES Combine dry ingredients in a medium bowl. In another bowl, whisk egg until frothy, then add 1 cup of the buttermilk and 1 tablespoon of the melted butter. Gradually add this liquid mixture to the dry ingredients and whisk until thoroughly incorporated. Puree ½ cup of the corn kernels, ½ cup of the raw nopalitos, and the remaining half cup buttermilk in a blender or food processor; fold into the batter, which should be the consistency of pancake batter. Stir in the remaining corn kernels, nopalitos, and chopped onions. Heat a small amount of the remaining butter in a heavy frying pan. Spoon batter into hot pan to form cakes 4 inches in diameter. When bottoms are lightly browned, flip to cook other side. Transfer to plate and keep warm while you continue the process, using butter as needed, until all the batter is cooked. You should have from 12 to 15 corn cakes.

8 large chicken thighs, deboned

1 tablespoon olive oil

1 teaspoon lemon pepper

CHICKEN THIGHS Coat chicken thighs with olive oil and sprinkle with lemon pepper. Grill or boil until done.

TO ASSEMBLE DISH Place 2 corn cakes on each plate, slightly overlapping. Slice chicken thinly. Arrange a fan of chicken slices on each corn cake. Top with Nopalito Chipotle Pumpkin Seed Sauce.

Chicken Yucatan

MAKES 4 TO 5 SERVINGS

Every meal on the Yucatan Peninsula of Mexico seems to be sparked with lime juice, from your drinks to your soup. Here is a modern adaptation of an ancient dish.

2 or 3 raw, cleaned prickly pear pads (page 25)

3½ pounds chicken breasts and thighs

½ cup flour, seasoned with salt and pepper

2 tablespoons vegetable oil

2 tablespoons butter

1 medium onion, thinly sliced

2 garlic cloves, minced

1 small can frozen orange-juice concentrate

Juice of 2 limes

¼ cup chopped green chiles

⅓ cup pine nuts (optional)

2 to 3 cups hot cooked rice

2 tablespoons chopped fresh cilantro or parsley

2 more limes, cut in slices or wedges

Cut prickly pear pads into strips about ½ inch wide. Cook according to directions of your choice on pages 26–27.

Wipe the chicken sections dry and dust lightly with seasoned flour. Heat the oil and butter together in one large skillet or two smaller ones. Add the chicken pieces, browning quickly on both sides. Add the onion and garlic and continue cooking for 5 minutes. Add the orange-juice concentrate and lime juice, turning chicken to distribute the sauce.

Reduce heat, cover the pan, and simmer gently for 10 minutes, adding a little water if sauce becomes dry. Remove the cover, add the green chiles, pine nuts if desired, and prickly pear strips. Re-cover and continue cooking until the chicken is done. Serve over hot cooked rice and sprinkle with the chopped cilantro or parsley. Place lime pieces around the edges.

Nopales y Pollo en Pimiento Dulce Rojo (Nopales and Chicken in Red Bell Pepper)

MAKES 2 SERVINGS

½ **cup olive oil**

1 **teaspoon minced cilantro**

1 **teaspoon minced onion**

¼ **teaspoon minced garlic**

4½ **teaspoons lemon juice**

2 **cleaned, raw prickly pear pads (page 25)**

1 **tablespoon olive oil**

2 **Holland red bell peppers**

¾ **cup of diced chicken breast meat (approximately 2 breasts, cut into ½ -inch squares)**

1 **tablespoon minced onion**

¼ **teaspoon minced garlic**

Salt and pepper

1⅓ **cups hot rice**

3 **cups shredded leaf lettuce**

¼ **cup cilantro leaves**

When I interviewed Suzana Dávila, owner and chef at Café Poca Cosa in Tucson, she didn't give me exact recipes; rather, she discussed recipe ideas—this stuffed pepper among them. Dávila comes from a Mexican restaurant family and is so inventive at putting together common ingredients in novel ways that she changes her menu twice a day to accommodate her creativity.

For this dish, be sure to use the thicker-walled Holland peppers as they have the right squat shape and are easier to peel without tearing.

Combine first 5 ingredients in blender jar and process until well combined to make dressing. Set aside. Cut prickly pear pads into ½-inch squares (nopalitos). Film a heavy frying pan with oil and roast the nopalitos slowly until they give up their juice, turning them over when they become olive-colored. Continue cooking for a few more minutes. The nopalitos will be slightly browned and will shrink. Transfer to a medium bowl.

Put red bell peppers under broiler or on grill, turning until all the skin is charred. Transfer to paper bag and let steam. In remaining olive oil, sauté chicken pieces with onion and garlic until no longer pink. Season with salt and pepper. Combine with nopalitos and mix with about half of dressing. Set aside.

Remove bell peppers from bag and very carefully remove skin and stems. It helps to do this under running water.

TO ASSEMBLE THE DISH On each of two plates, make a bed of hot rice about 5 inches in diameter. Center a pepper on the rice and fill with half of the chicken and nopalito mixture. Distribute shredded lettuce around the pepper and drizzle with remaining dressing. Garnish with cilantro leaves.

Grilled Chicken with Nopalito and Pineapple Salsa

MAKES 4 SERVINGS

1 raw, cleaned prickly pear pad (page 25)

1 tablespoon vegetable oil

1 cup canned crushed pineapple packed in its own juice

¼ cup finely chopped red bell pepper

¼ cup thinly sliced green onions, including some tops

1 tablespoon chopped canned green chiles

1 finely minced serrano chile (optional)

½ teaspoon finely minced garlic

2 tablespoons lime juice

¼ teaspoon salt

1 tablespoon finely minced cilantro (optional)

4 large boneless chicken breasts

8 medium-size flour tortillas

4 cups finely shredded leaf lettuce

This makes a delicious light entrée when served as a stuffing for warm flour tortillas. It can also be served with rice and a vegetable.

Cut prickly pear pad in 1½-inch squares. Film a heavy frying pan with the oil and add the prickly pear pads. Cook over low heat, turning occasionally, until pieces have given up much of their juice and are slightly brown. Remove from pan, cool, and chop into pieces as wide as a matchstick and about ¼ inch long.

Transfer to medium bowl. Add remaining ingredients (except for chicken), stir to combine, and set aside for flavors to mingle.

Grill chicken breasts until done. Warm tortillas while you slice each chicken breast crosswise into eight pieces. Divide chicken and lettuce evenly among the tortillas and top with salsa. Fold tortillas to enclose stuffing.

Carne Asada con Nopales y Tomatillo

MAKES 1 SERVING

¼ to ⅓ **pound skirt steak, flank steak, or top round steak**

Italian dressing

Juice of 2 or 3 fresh limes

Raw, cleaned prickly pear pads (page 25), about twice as much as you have of the steak

Olive or vegetable oil

2 thick slices of onion

2 thick slices of tomato

4 cups of cooked rice

Tomatillo Sauce (recipe follows)

Suzana Dávila, chef-owner of Café Poca Cosa restaurant in downtown Tucson, does not cook from recipes—she cooks from inspiration. When we sat down in the early morning calm of her spectacularly colorful restaurant, she spun this idea out, inventing as she spoke. The idea is hers, the details are mine. This barbecue dish can be expanded to as much as your grill can hold. Serve the steak, vegetables, and sauce on a bed of rice, with warm flour or corn tortillas on the side.

Marinate steak in a mixture of the Italian dressing and lime juice. Brush prickly pear pads on both sides with a little oil. Grill about 5 minutes on each side, until color changes, juices sizzle, and there is some browning. Move to side of grill to keep warm while you grill steak, onion, and tomato.

TO ASSEMBLE DISH Slice steak thinly, slice prickly pear pads into strips roughly the same size as the steak strips. On platter, make a bed of rice. Top with tomatillo sauce and arrange steak, prickly pear pads, tomato, and onions on top.

MAKES ENOUGH FOR 6 TO 8 SERVINGS

1 onion, chopped

1 teaspoon chopped garlic

1 tablespoon olive oil

4 cups chopped tomatillos (husks removed, about 1¼ pounds)

½ **cup chicken stock**

1 to 2 small jalapeños (optional)

¼ **cup chopped green Anaheim chiles**

TOMATILLO SAUCE In medium saucepan over low heat, sauté onion and garlic in olive oil until translucent. Add chopped tomatillos and chicken stock. Using rubber gloves, slit the jalapeños, remove seeds and membranes, and chop fine. Add jalapeños and Anaheim chiles to tomatillo mixture and simmer until tomatillos are tender.

Beef with Prickly Pear and Port Sauce

MAKES 4 SERVINGS

1 shallot, minced (2 to 2½ tablespoons)

1 cup Port wine

½ cup prickly pear syrup, bottled or homemade (page 30)

Juice of 1 lemon

Juice of 1 orange

2 teaspoons red-wine vinegar

Dash of cayenne pepper

Salt and pepper to taste

Zest of 1 orange, slivered

1½ pounds beef or venison steak

This dish could also be called Red on Red, a glorious red sauce for red meat. The recipe comes from noted New York author and cooking teacher Perla Myers. Don't be tempted to leave out the cayenne—it delivers an important flavor note. Should you have access to venison, this sauce will stand up to the hearty flavor of the meat. Not a meat eater? It's good on chicken too.

Combine shallots and Port in small saucepan over medium heat. Simmer until liquid is reduced by half. Add prickly pear syrup, citrus juices, vinegar, and spices, and simmer for 5 minutes. Add the slivered orange zest and simmer for another 3 minutes. Set aside. Fry or broil steak, and slice thin to serve. Serve with room-temperature sauce.

Diabetics should use homemade prickly pear syrup or Arizona Cactus Ranch prickly pear nectar, which is unsweetened.

Prickly Pear Pork Tenderloin

MAKES 4 SERVINGS

This recipe comes from Alan Zeman, chef and owner of Fuego restaurant in Tucson. In addition to cooking up innovative dishes, Zeman has hosted a radio talk show called The Dinner Hour, *has written a quarterly food column, and sells his own line of Southwestern condiments.*

Chef Zeman serves this dish with sweet-potato fries and sautéed petite vegetables.

4 portions of pork tenderloin, 6 ounces apiece

1 tablespoon unsalted Sonoran Seasoning*

¼ cup applejack

½ cup veal stock or beef stock

1½ cups Prickly Pear Barbecue Glaze*

1 cup shredded savoy cabbage

½ teaspoon olive oil

¼ cup Onion Marmalade (recipe follows)

¼ cup balsamic vinegar

¼ cup prepared Spicy Apple Chutney (recipe follows)

Season pork tenderloins with Sonoran Seasoning and sear in hot frying pan until nicely browned. Add applejack, heat, and remove from heat. Flambé according to directions at the end of this recipe. Deglaze pan with stock and simmer, covered, about 10 minutes until just cooked. Add Prickly Pear Glaze to reduced liquid and reduce again. Set aside and keep warm.

Sear cabbage in small frying pan in olive oil. Add Onion Marmalade and balsamic vinegar and simmer several minutes until tender.

TO ASSEMBLE DISH Slice pork tenderloin portions and fan on each plate in a horseshoe pattern. Place braised cabbage in horseshoe and top with 1 tablespoon or more Spicy Apple Chutney. Drizzle some of the sauce over the meat.

MAKES ABOUT ¾ CUP

2 onions, quartered and sliced

¼ cup chicken stock

2 tablespoons brandy

ONION MARMALADE In a nonstick skillet, combine onions and stock. Cook down slowly until onions are pasty and browned (this takes about an hour). Stir in brandy. Cool and refrigerate if made ahead. Will last several days in the refrigerator.

MAKES 1 1/2 PINTS

2 pounds apples, peeled and diced

1/2 cup brown sugar

1 cup cider vinegar

1 small onion, diced

1/2 teaspoon chopped garlic

1/4 teaspoon ground cloves

1/4 teaspoon ground allspice

1/2 teaspoon red chile flakes

SPICY APPLE CHUTNEY Combine all ingredients in a saucepot. Bring to a boil, then turn down heat and simmer approximately 1 hour until liquid evaporates, forming a nice glazed sauce. Cool and refrigerate if made ahead. Will last several weeks in the refrigerator.

TO FLAMBÉ For safety, use a kitchen mitt to hold the pan, and make sure there is nothing flammable above the pan when you set it aflame. Make sure your hair is not loose, and avoid wearing loose or long sleeves during this process. Tilt the pan so liquid gathers on one side of pan, then carefully light the liqueur with a long wooden match, averting your eyes as it first flames up. This process will burn off the alcohol, but the flavor of the liqueur remains.

* See Sources (page 116) for these products. You can substitute Prickly Pear Barbecue Sauce (page 73 or 116) for the Prickly Pear Barbecue Glaze. For the Sonoran Seasoning you can substitute a mixture of 1 teaspoon each mild chile powder and finely ground dried orange peel, 1/4 teaspoon each granulated garlic, granulated onion, and black pepper, and 1/8 teaspoon each celery seed and sugar. The results, of course, will be somewhat altered in flavor.

Fish in Nopalito Shrimp Sauce

MAKES 6 SERVINGS

2 small prickly pear pads, cleaned (page 25)

$1/2$ teaspoon cooking oil

1 small jalapeño

2 tablespoons olive oil

$1/4$ cup finely chopped onion

2 tablespoons finely chopped shallots

$1/3$ cup chopped red bell pepper

1 tablespoon lemon juice

$1/2$ cup chicken broth

12 medium shrimp, cleaned and chopped, or $1/2$ pound baby shrimp

$1/2$ teaspoon salt

$1/2$ teaspoon pepper

$1^{1}/2$ teaspoons cornstarch

6 portions firm fish fillets (4 to 6 ounces each)

Every year the Texas Cactus Council sponsors a cook-off during which cactus lovers compete with their best recipes using prickly pear pads. In 1996, Abel Villareal, of Corpus Christi, a frequent contestant, won second place in the main-dish category for this dish. I tried it with salmon, and it was delicious; other firm fish fillets will work as well.

Cut prickly pear pads into pieces 2 inches square. Arrange pieces in a heavy frying pan sprayed or brushed with cooking oil. Cook over medium heat until the nopalitos (the chopped prickly pear pads) have lost the bright green color and are somewhat shrunken, an indication that some of the sticky juice has dried up. Turn off heat and set aside. When cool, cut into $1/4$-inch dice. Halve jalapeño, scrape out seeds and ribs. Chop fine and set aside.

Heat olive oil in a two-quart saucepan over medium heat. Sauté onions, shallots, and bell pepper until onions are translucent. Add jalapeño, nopalitos, lemon juice, and chicken broth, and simmer gently for 5 minutes.

Add chopped shrimp, salt, and pepper, and cook until shrimp are just pink. Mix cornstarch with about a tablespoon of water and stir in. Simmer for 3 minutes. Keep sauce warm while you grill or sauté the fish fillets.

Spoon a little sauce on each of six plates. Top with fish fillet and spoon more sauce over fish.

Prickly Pear Barbecue Shrimp with Roasted Corn and Black Bean Relish

MAKES 2 TO 4 SERVINGS, DEPENDING ON SIZE OF SHRIMP

2 medium ears sweet corn

12 large shrimp, cleaned

Salt and freshly ground black pepper to taste

3 tablespoons olive oil

1 cup cooked black beans

1 cup Prickly Pear Barbecue Glaze (recipe follows)

¼ cup chopped fresh cilantro

This dish was developed by Richard Sederholt, the award-winning chef at Remington's at the Scottsdale Plaza Resort. Remington's, which takes its name from its numerous bronze sculptures by Western artist Frederick Remington, offers guests the option of patio dining with dramatic views of Phoenix-area landmark Camelback Mountain. The recipe makes four small servings if the shrimp are very large. If the shrimp are small to medium, count on 2 generous servings.

Husk the corn and roast it on a grill or under a broiler until some of the kernels are light brown. Cool and cut the corn from the cob. You should have about a cup. Season the cleaned shrimp with salt and pepper. Heat the oil in a medium sauté pan and sauté the shrimp for several minutes until they turn pink and are cooked through. Remove shrimp from pan. Add roasted corn and black beans to the pan and sauté for several minutes until heated through. Add Prickly Pear Barbecue Glaze and toss. Finish heating the shrimp through, being careful not to overcook. Transfer the bean and corn mixture to a serving dish to make a bed and arrange shrimp on top. Garnish with cilantro.

¼ cup sugar

¼ cup red-wine vinegar

½ teaspoon lemon juice

¼ cup prickly pear syrup or jelly (pages 30, 72, 116)

1 cup chicken stock or broth

1½ teaspoons Southwestern Seasoning (recipe follows)

2½ teaspoons cornstarch mixed with 1 tablespoon water (for thickening)

PRICKLY PEAR BARBECUE GLAZE Combine sugar, red-wine vinegar, and lemon juice in a sauce pot, and simmer over medium heat until it has reduced by three-quarters and is lightly caramelized. There will be bubbles throughout the sauce rather than just on top. Add the prickly pear syrup or jelly, the chicken stock, and the seasoning and bring to a boil. Add cornstarch and water paste and simmer for another minute. Cool. The glaze will keep for up to a week in the refrigerator.

CHEF RICK'S SOUTHWESTERN SEASONING Mix 3 parts chile powder with one part each granulated garlic, ground cumin, gumbo filé powder, Mexican oregano, ground black pepper, cayenne pepper, ground cinnamon, ground allspice, paprika, onion powder, dried basil, kosher salt, ground nutmeg, and dried thyme. Mix all ingredients together. If you prefer a hotter seasoning, you can increase the cayenne pepper.

SERVES 2 TO 4

Nopal Frittata

**4 raw, cleaned prickly pear
pads (page 25)**

2 tablespoons butter

2 small tomatoes

**2 thin slices red onion, sliced
horizontally to make rings**

6 eggs

$1/2$ teaspoon salt

**$1/4$ teaspoon freshly
ground black pepper**

**$1/2$ cup grated Monterey Jack or any
Mexican cheese**

Nopalitos and eggs is a classic Mexican dish—just as common as ham and eggs in a U.S. coffee shop. It can be made simply with squares of prickly pear pads and beaten eggs fried in a little oil or butter. This slightly more elaborate version makes a good brunch or lunch dish.

Cut each prickly pear pad into pieces about 1 inch square. Melt $1/2$ teaspoon butter in medium frying pan and add the cactus pieces. Cook over low heat, letting the juices evaporate. Meanwhile, slice tomatoes and separate onion into rings. When cactus pieces are slightly brown, push to one side. Melt remaining butter, evenly distribute cactus over bottom of pan, and layer the onion rings and tomatoes on top.

Preheat broiler. Cover pan for 1 or 2 minutes to slightly cook and warm tomato and onion. Crack eggs into medium bowl and whisk until golden. Season with salt and pepper. Uncover pan and add beaten eggs. Cook over low heat until just set, lifting edges of cooked egg with spatula and tilting pan to let uncooked egg run underneath. Sprinkle with grated cheese. Put under broiler to brown slightly. Cut into wedges and serve with salsa and warm corn or flour tortillas.

MAKES 4 VEGETARIAN MAIN-DISH
SERVINGS OR 6 SIDE-DISH SERVINGS

¼ cup olive oil, divided

2 medium eggplants (about 1 pound),
cut into ½-inch dice

2 medium onions cut into ½-inch dice

4 medium zucchini (about 1½
pounds), cut into ½-inch dice

2 medium red bell peppers, cored,
seeded, and cut into ½-inch dice

2 raw, cleaned prickly pear pads, cut
into pieces about 1 inch square

4 cloves of garlic, minced

4 ripe Roma tomatoes,
cut into small dice

1 cup tomato purée

4 sprigs fresh thyme

1 bay leaf

Salt to taste

Nopalito Ratatouille

Barry Infuso is a chef, cooking teacher, and food consultant. He has a master's degree in nutritional anthropology as well as a culinary degree, but learned to cook informally during summers spent with his Italian grandmother. Infuso developed this recipe while consulting for the Yaqui Indian tribe in Arizona. The Yaquis are prone to diabetes, and since nopalitos have been shown to regulate blood sugar, the tribe's medical personnel were seeking suggestions for incorporating the cactus into the diets of their patients. This versatile dish can be served hot as a side dish or used as a sauce for pasta. It is also delicious served cold as a salad.

Heat 2 tablespoons of olive oil in a large Dutch oven. Add the eggplant and cook over medium heat, stirring to prevent overcooking, until golden brown, about 10 minutes. Transfer eggplant to a bowl and set aside.

Add the remaining 2 tablespoons of oil to the pan and heat. Add the onion and cook until translucent. Add the zucchini and cook until tender. Add the peppers, cactus, garlic, tomatoes, purée, thyme, bay leaf, and salt. Simmer for 10 minutes or until tomato falls apart. Return eggplant to dish, stir, and continue to cook uncovered for 15 minutes. Remove the bay leaf and thyme. Adjust seasoning.

Southwestern Casserole

MAKES 6 TO 8 SERVINGS

- 8 cleaned prickly pear pads (page 25)
- 4 cups of refried beans (mashed pinto beans)
- 2 cups enchilada sauce (canned or homemade)
- 1 to 1½ cups grated Monterey Jack or asadero cheese

This is a traditional Lenten dish in Mexico and the Southwest, where many Catholics observe dietary restrictions before Easter.

Prepare prickly pear pads according to your choice of directions (pages 26–27).

Preheat oven to 350 degrees. Spread each pad with beans and arrange in a flat casserole dish about 10 x 14 inches, making two layers if necessary. Cover with enchilada sauce. Top with grated cheese.

Bake for 15 to 20 minutes until the sauce is bubbling and cheese is melted.

Peruvian Nopalito Rice

MAKES ABOUT 8 SIDE-DISH SERVINGS

- 1 pound brown rice
- 1 tablespoon oil
- 4 cups water
- 1 cup finely chopped onion
- 2 cups nopalitos, cleaned (page 25) and cut into ¼-inch dice
- Pinch of oregano
- Sprinkle of garlic salt
- 1 tablespoon chopped pimiento

Every Labor Day, David Eppele of Arizona Cactus and Succulent Research in Bisbee, Arizona, hosted a fiesta for friends and fed them on cactus (see his recipe for El Jefe's Cactus Wine, page 39). One year Adelita Gomez, a guest all the way from Lima, Peru, contributed this recipe from her homeland.

In large heavy saucepan, sauté rice in oil until coated. Add water, onion, nopalitos, oregano, and garlic salt. Cook over very low heat about 40 minutes or until rice is tender. Stir in pimiento.

CACTUS HONEY SHERBET

SUNSET SORBET

PRICKLY PEAR–BERRY GELATO

DESERT DAWN PIE

JEWEL PIE

SABRA SOUFFLÉ

NOPALITOS WITH HONEY

FLAMBÉED PRICKLY PEARS

PRICKLY PEAR TIRAMISÙ

MAKES ABOUT 1 QUART

Cactus Honey Sherbet (See photo on page 105, left)

3 medium very ripe peaches

1 envelope unflavored gelatin

¼ cup cold water

2½ cups prickly pear purée or juice (page 29) or Arizona Cactus Ranch nectar

½ cup honey

5 tablespoons lemon juice

½ cup whipping cream

Both peaches and prickly pears ripen from mid-summer to early fall, depending on where you live. What better time to make this rosy ice cream that combines the mellow flavors of both fruits?

Plunge the peaches into a large pot of boiling water for one minute; using a slotted spoon, transfer them immediately to a large bowl of cold water. The skins should slip off easily. Slice the peaches. This should make about 1½ cups.

Sprinkle gelatin over the ¼ cup cold water in a small bowl. Set aside. Combine 1 cup prickly pear purée, juice, or nectar with peach slices in a medium saucepan. Simmer over low heat for 5 minutes.

Turn off the heat under the fruit, strain off 1 cup of liquid. In a small saucepan, combine this liquid with the honey, and cook gently just at a simmer until honey is dissolved. Remove from heat. Add the softened gelatin and lemon juice to the honey mixture and stir until gelatin is dissolved.

Purée the cooked peaches and remaining juice in a blender. Combine with the gelatin and honey mixture and—if you have an ice-cream maker—the whipping cream. Refrigerate until chilled. Pour into the container of your ice-cream maker. Process according to manufacturer's directions until mixture is hard to churn. Remove dasher. Cover and freeze for an hour or 2.

If you don't have an ice-cream maker, transfer mixture to plastic bowl before adding whipping cream, and freeze until nearly hard. Break up and beat with an electric mixer. Beat the whipping cream until stiff and fold into the fruit mixture. Refreeze until firm.

MAKES ABOUT 1 QUART

Sunset Sorbet

1 envelope unflavored gelatin

1 cup orange juice

$1/4$ cup sugar (or equivalent non-nutritive sweetener)

2 cups prickly pear juice (page 29)

$1/2$ cup lime juice

2 tablespoons tequila

1 tablespoon Triple Sec

This sorbet can serve as a dessert (adults only!) or as a palate refresher between courses. The alcohol lowers the point at which the mixture will freeze, so add it only at the end.

In a small bowl, soften the gelatin in $1/2$ cup of the orange juice. In a medium saucepan, heat the remaining orange juice to boiling. Remove from heat and add the softened gelatin and the sugar and stir until dissolved. Let cool.

Add the prickly pear juice and lime juice to the orange juice mixture and pour into a 1-quart (or larger) container of an ice cream maker. Process according to manufacturer's directions until sorbet becomes hard to churn. Add the tequila and Triple Sec and process until firm. Serve, or to further firm and mellow, cover and freeze for 1 to 2 hours.

MAKES ABOUT 1 QUART

Prickly Pear–Berry Gelato

12 medium prickly pears or 1 cup purée (see page 29)

2 cups (scant) strawberries or frozen mixed berries

1 tablespoon lemon juice

$1/3$ to $1/2$ cup sugar or equivalent

2 tablespoons cornstarch

2 strips lemon peel (yellow part only), about 2 inches long and $1/2$ inch wide

2 cups 1% or 2% milk

2 teaspoons vanilla

Gelato is a creamy frozen concoction popular in Italy, where prickly pear fruits are popular as well. Traditional gelato is made rich with eggs. This version starts with a cooked base but substitutes cornstarch for egg yolks. This cooked base keeps the texture creamy as the gelato freezes.

Clean, peel, and seed prickly pears (see pages 28–29). Whirl in food processor or blender to purée. You should have about 1 cup. Wash and trim strawberries and purée in blender or food processor with the lemon juice. Set aside.

In a medium saucepan, combine sugar, cornstarch, and lemon peel, first squeezing or twisting the peel to release oils. Stir in milk. Over medium heat, bring mixture to a boil, stirring with wire whisk to break up any lumps. Boil 1 minute, continuing to stir. Remove from heat and discard lemon peel.

Stir prickly pear and berry purées into the hot mixture until incorporated. Add vanilla. Transfer to a bowl and cool. Taste to see if it needs more sweetening; if so, stir in additional sugar or equivalent. Cover and refrigerate until cold, at least $1^1/2$ hours or until the next day.

Pour into the container of your ice-cream maker. Process according to manufacturer's directions until mixture is hard to stir. Remove dasher. Cover and freeze for an hour or 2. To serve, briefly soften in refrigerator until gelato can be scooped.

MAKES ONE 9-INCH PIE

Desert Dawn Pie

3 eggs

³/₄ cup prickly pear juice (page 29)

¹/₄ cup sugar

1 envelope unflavored gelatin

1 cup heavy cream

¹/₄ cup frozen orange-juice concentrate

4 or 5 drops yellow food coloring

1 baked 9-inch piecrust

Note: The chances of contracting illness from raw eggs is very small. But to avoid risk, use only clean AA-grade eggs that are extremely fresh and have been consistently refrigerated. The very young, the elderly, and those with immune-system diseases should not eat raw eggs.

Slices of this pie will reveal layers of deep pink and rich gold similar to the sky at dawn over the desert. The directions may seem long, but the procedure is not complicated.

Separate eggs, placing whites in a small deep bowl and yolks in the top part of a double boiler. Beat yolks; add prickly pear juice, sugar, and gelatin. Cook in the top part of the double boiler over simmering water until gelatin is dissolved and mixture thickens. (If you do not have a double boiler, you can try this in a regular saucepan, but use low heat and stir constantly. If you are not very careful, and worse yet, if you let the mixture boil, you will have little bits of scrambled egg in your sauce.)

Transfer mixture to a small bowl and chill until it begins to form a soft peak or mound when stirred—at least 1 hour.

While the juice mixture is chilling, beat the egg whites until stiff. Whip the cream in a deep bowl until stiff. Fold egg whites and whipped cream together. Transfer about a cup of this mixture to a small bowl. Add 2 tablespoons of orange-juice concentrate and stir gently to incorporate. Add yellow food coloring until mixture is brilliant and fold it all together.

Now add the thickened, chilled juice mixture to the remaining egg whites and whipped-cream mixture and fold together gently. Add the remaining 2 tablespoons of the orange-juice concentrate and fold together until well combined.

Mound about half of the pink mixture into the piecrust. Add four big dollops of the yellow mixture, then pile on the remaining pink mixture and add any remaining yellow mixture to the top. With the edge of a spatula, swirl through the two colors once to make a marbled effect.

Chill until firm.

MAKES ONE 8-INCH PIE

Jewel Pie

¾ cup apple juice

2½ tablespoons cornstarch

¾ cup prickly pear juice (page 29)

¼ cup honey (or more, to taste)

5 medium peaches or a 29-ounce can of sliced peaches

1 baked 9- or 10-inch piecrust

This pie resembles chunks of amber floating in a ruby-red sauce. It is especially lovely if you make the piecrust in a fluted quiche pan with a removable bottom.

Combine ¼ cup of the apple juice and the cornstarch in a small bowl. Set aside. Combine prickly pear juice, remaining apple juice, and honey in a saucepan and heat until honey is melted. Add cornstarch mixture and cook and stir over medium heat until mixture comes to a boil and thickens. Cook one minute. Set aside to cool.

Bring a medium pot of water to boil over high heat. Immerse peaches for one minute in the boiling water, then remove with a slotted spoon to a bowl of cold water. Peels will slip off. Slice peaches in uniform slices and arrange, pinwheel fashion, in two concentric circles in the pie shell.

Pour glaze (thickened juice) over peaches. Refrigerate for four hours before serving. If you've used a pie pan with a removable bottom, take the pie from the pan and position on a pretty plate.

MAKES 4 TO 6 SERVINGS

Sabra Soufflé

2 cups prickly pear fruits, peeled and seeded (see pages 28–29)

½ cup orange juice

½ cup tequila or vodka

1 tablespoon lemon juice

½ cup milk

1 vanilla bean

3 tablespoons butter

3 tablespoons flour

4 egg yolks

6 egg whites

¼ teaspoon salt

6 tablespoons sugar

Daniel Rogov developed this recipe to use prickly pears, which are popular in Israel. Rogov is the restaurant and wine critic for the daily Israeli newspaper HaAretz *as well as for the Israeli version of* The International Herald Tribune. *He contributes regularly to European newspapers and magazines. The prickly pear fruit is called a* sabra *in Israel. Native-born Israelis are also called* sabras—*prickly on the outside, sweet on the inside.*

Preheat oven to 350 degrees. Slice the prickly pear fruits, placing slices in a small bowl. Combine the orange juice, tequila or vodka, and lemon juice in another small bowl and pour over the prickly pear slices. Stir well and let stand for 1 hour. Pour off ½ cup of the liquid and reserve.

In a small saucepan, combine the milk and the reserved liquid. Add the vanilla bean. Bring slowly to a boil and simmer for several seconds. Remove from heat and remove vanilla bean. Set mixture aside.

In a large heavy saucepan, melt the butter over low heat. Add the flour and cook, stirring constantly, for 3 minutes without allowing it to brown. Pour the scalded milk mixture into this pan, stirring briskly while simmering for 4 to 5 minutes until the mixture thickens. Turn off heat and allow to cool a little while you prepare the eggs.

Beat egg yolks in a small bowl. Set aside. In another bowl, beat egg whites with salt until stiff. Add a little of the milk mixture to the egg yolks and beat. Slowly add remaining milk mixture, beating constantly. (You must warm egg yolks slowly, or they will curdle.) Fold the beaten egg whites into the mixture.

Arrange the prickly pear slices in the bottom of an 8-inch soufflé dish, and over these, pour the extra liquid. Cover with the soufflé batter and bake for 20 minutes. Sprinkle the sugar on top and bake about 10 minutes longer. Serve immediately.

MAKES 4 SERVINGS

Nopalitos with Honey

¼ cup butter

6 small prickly pear pads, cleaned and cut into thin strips (see page 25)

½ cup honey

1 teaspoon lemon juice

3 tablespoons warm water

3 tablespoons anisette, arak, or ouzo liqueur

¼ cup pine nuts

This recipe for a popular Israeli dessert comes from Israeli food writer Daniel Rogov.

In a skillet, melt the butter and sauté the nopalito strips, turning once, for 1 minute.

In a small bowl, combine the honey and lemon juice with the warm water. Pour this mixture over the nopalitos and cook over a low flame for 1 minute longer. Add the liqueur and cook for 2 more minutes. Sprinkle with the pine nuts and serve hot.

Flambéed Prickly Pears

MAKES 1 SERVING; EXPAND AS NECESSARY

3 prickly pears, peeled and seeded (see page 25)

1½ teaspoons butter

1 teaspoon brown sugar

Dash of powdered cardamom

2 tablespoons Sabra or Grand Marnier liqueur

2 tablespoons whipped cream

This recipe comes from Israeli chef Tsachi Buchester, a television and media figure in that part of the world. When he opened his Tel Aviv restaurant—The Pink Ladle—in the 1980s, he became one of the first chefs to feature nouvelle cuisine based largely on unique combinations of local ingredients. Prickly pears grow widely in Israel and are a popular fresh fruit there.

Slice the prickly pears. In a skillet, melt half the butter, add the sugar and cardamom, and in this sauté the prickly pear slices for 1 minute. Add the liqueur, let it warm through for a few seconds, and then remove from heat and flambé according to directions below. When the flames die down, add the remaining butter and let melt. Arrange in a small glass dish or cocktail glass and top with whipped cream. Serve warm or cool.

TO FLAMBÉ For safety, use a kitchen mitt to hold the pan, and make sure there is nothing flammable above the pan when you set it aflame. Make sure your hair is not loose, and avoid wearing loose or long sleeves during this process. Tilt the pan so liquid gathers on one side of pan, then carefully light the liqueur with a long wooden match, averting your eyes as it first flames up. This process will burn off the alcohol, but the flavor of the liqueur remains.

SERVES 8

Prickly Pear Tiramisù

2 large eggs, separated
$1/3$ cup powdered sugar
1 pound mascarpone cheese
2 cups heavy cream
$1/4$ cup prickly pear fruit purée (page 29)
1 cup espresso, chilled
$1/2$ cup Marsala wine
1 tablespoon rum
1 pound ladyfingers or savoiardi
2 ounces semisweet chocolate, grated

Note: The chances of contracting illness from raw eggs is very small. But to avoid risk, use only clean AA-grade eggs that are extremely fresh and have been consistently refrigerated. The very young, the elderly, and those with immune-system diseases should not eat raw eggs.

The food at Medizona, a cozy Scottsdale restaurant, combines the traditions of the Southwestern United States and the Mediterranean area. Esquire *magazine named it the best new restaurant in America in 2000, and critics have declared the food "not for the unadventurous." This prickly pear tiramisù is one of Medizona's signature dishes. The prickly pear flavor is very mild, and this dish uses crispy ladyfingers called* savoiardi, *available in Italian delicatessens. For a stronger cactus flavor, try my variation.*

Beat egg yolks with sugar in bowl with electric mixer until lighter colored and fluffy. Add mascarpone and incorporate. In another bowl, beat egg whites until stiff. Gently fold in mascarpone mixture. Set aside.

In small, deep bowl, beat cream until stiff, add prickly pear purée, and beat until stiff again. Gently fold prickly pear whipped cream into mascarpone mixture until totally incorporated. Set aside.

Combine espresso, Marsala, and rum in bowl. Dip in ladyfingers one at a time and arrange in two side-by-side rows in a 9 x 12-inch dish. Drizzle a little more espresso mixture over the ladyfingers. Cover with half the mascarpone mixture. Dip the remaining ladyfingers, arrange on the mascarpone, and cover with other half of the mascarpone mixture. Cover with plastic wrap and refrigerate at least 6 hours or overnight. Sprinkle with grated chocolate just before serving.

VARIATION To modify the traditional tiramisù flavor with something fruitier, dip the savoiardi in a mixture of half Marsala wine or a fruit wine and half prickly pear syrup or purée.

SOURCES

PRICKLY PEAR FRUIT JUICE, SYRUPS, NECTAR, AND SAUCES

Cheri Romanowski
Cheri's Desert Harvest
800-743-1141
www.cherisdesertharvest.com
Cheri's Desert Harvest, located in Tucson, offers a selection of prickly pear jellies and syrups. Cheri is a stickler for freshness and quality. Call or order from website.

Natalie McGee
Arizona Cactus Ranch
P.O. Box 8
Green Valley, AZ 85622
520-625-4419
800-582-9903
www.arizonacactusranch.com
Unsweetened prickly pear nectar (excellent product for diabetics), jam, and other products. Call or order from website.

Chef Alan Zeman's
Southwestern Originals
P.O. Box 31283
Tucson, AZ 85751
Ph. 520-886-1745
Fax 520-886-6084
www.fuegorestaurant.com
Prickly Pear Barbecue Glaze, Sonoran Seasoning, and other products. Call or write for order form, or order from website.

PRICKLY PEAR PADS

John Dicus
Rivenrock Gardens
www.rivenrock.com
Organically grown, nearly spineless prickly pear pads in several grades. Picked fresh the day they are shipped and worth the price. Order from website. Also carries ornamental landscape cactus.

CHILES

Native Seeds/SEARCH
526 North Fourth Avenue
Tucson, AZ 85705
520-622-5561
www.nativeseeds.org
A nonprofit conservation organization working to preserve traditional crop varieties of peoples of the American Southwest and northwest Mexico. Offers chile seeds, diverse chiles, and chile powder. They also carry prickly pear products. Catalog for $1.

Santa Cruz Chili and
Spice Company
1868 East Frontage Road
P.O. Box 177
Tumacacori, AZ 85640
520-398-2591
www.santacruzchili.com
For decades this small company has been supplying people across the country with high-quality chile products of all kinds.

FOR MORE INFORMATION ON CACTUS

Texas Cactus Council
P.O. Box 423
Benavides, TX 78341
Sponsors an annual cactus cookoff during which members and guests showcase their favorite recipes for prickly pear pads and fruits. The council also does a monthly newsletter.

INDEX